AF266270

Three-in-One
Low Carb Lifestyle
Cooking Booklets

LC15 Series

Includes the first three booklets published as eBooks in the series:
Mexican Food for a Low Carb Lifestyle
Breakfast Choices for a Low Carb Lifestyle
Magic Muffins for a Low Carb Lifestyle

Rene Averett

Other Books by Rene Averett

Low Carb Recipe Magic
Books in this series:
Meals for Two – Book 1
Sweets by the Season – Book 2

Copyright © 2017 Rene Averett

All photos were taken by Rene Averett
Cover Design by Rene Averett
Low Carb 15 Series™ is a trademark of Pynhavyn Press
First Edition: September 2017

Published through Pynhavyn Press
(www.pynhavyn.com)

All rights reserved.

Introduction

I have been a yo-yo dieter for most of my life, and I learned a lot about how to lose weight and how to gain it. How to keep it off is the trick. Add to that, how to keep it off while still enjoying the foods I love is the challenge. I knew that if I couldn't find a way to enjoy my favorite foods while still maintaining a very low carb lifestyle, then I would fail once again to keep the weight under control.

Let's face it, I love food. I love sweets. I love bread. These are part of what makes life so pleasurable. And I love Mexican food, which led to my first LC15 booklet. Mexican food is filled with high carbohydrate ingredients such as corn, flour, beans, rice, sugar, and tomatoes, so you have to use substitutes for what you can. Use the rest of the ingredients in moderation to make a dish that is low in effective carbohydrates.

We have some help with tortillas that are low carb and made commercially. *La Tortilla Factory* makes a 6" whole-wheat tortilla that tastes very good and only has 3 net carbs in it. They also make a burrito-sized one with 5 net carbs. They have a flour tortilla that is about 7" and checks in at 6 net carbs that is good for larger wraps. Several more companies are now making low carbs tortillas and wraps.

The Breakfast Choices booklet came from people asking about breakfast recipes and what they could eat to stay on their low carb diet. Many possible breakfast options are available, and I've only given you a few. My blog has even more recipes. You can find it at www.reneaverett.me/skinnygirl/

Magic Muffins are a variation of a recipe I found on the Atkins Diet site. I adapted in many ways to create a variety of muffins that you can make in a microwave or convection oven. You can even use a toaster oven. When they are prepared in different ways, they change taste and texture, which makes them versatile as well as easy to make for one person.

Really, with a low carb diet, the choice of low carb flours and sugar-free products that are available, you can have your cake and eat it, too. Because low carb doesn't have to be boring.

Now for a bit of a disclaimer. I have a list of flour and other ingredients I use that are made for low carb. All low carb products are not created equal, so be sure to check the net carb count of the flours, sugars, jams, etc. that you use and adjust the carb counts if needed. The carb counts will vary slightly based on products used and serving sizes, so while they may be close, they may be a little bit more or less.

Rene Averett, August 2017

Contents

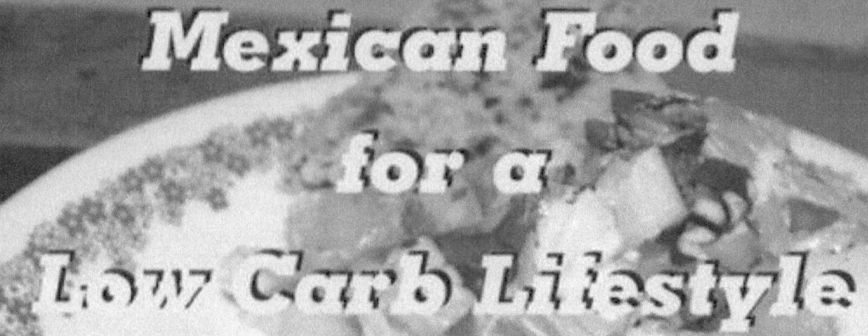

15 Fabulous Recipes
under 10 net carbs each

Rene Averett

Author of Low Carb Recipe Magic Series

Mexican Food for a Low Carb Lifestyle

Low Carb 15 Series

Rene Averett

Albondigas Soup

A favorite Mexican-style meatball soup with spices and chiles in it. Very
tasty. I added a pan-grilled low carb tortilla with cheese on the side.

20 one-inch Meatballs (homemade or frozen)
22 oz. Beef broth
1/2 cup Carrots, diced
1/2 cup Celery, finely chopped
1 15-oz can chopped Tomatoes
1 4-oz. can Green Chiles, diced
1/2 cup Daikon Radish shredded
1 tablespoon Cayenne Pepper
1/4 teaspoon Seasoning Salt
1/2 teaspoon dried Cilantro or Parsley

Look for low carb meatballs. Many are made with breadcrumbs or make
your own from one pound of ground beef.

If meatballs are not precooked, then cook them in the oven or in a pan until
almost done. Remove and let cool.

In a medium saucepan, add beef broth, carrots, tomatoes, chiles, and
daikon radish and bring to a boil. Add seasonings, then lower to a simmer.

Add the meatballs, cover, and let cook for about 30 minutes until the carrots are tender. Taste the broth to check the seasonings and adjust as needed.

Serve in a bowl with a tortilla or a quesadilla on the side. Sprinkle with cheese if desired. Makes 4 servings, 5 meatballs each.

Nutrition Information per serving:
Calories: 355 Fat:23.9 g Net Carbs: 8.8 g Protein: 23.6 g

Quesadilla

For the uninitiated, a quesadilla is simply a cheese-filled tortilla that is pan-fried in a skillet. To make one, use a low carb tortilla. Warm it to soften it, then put about 1/4 cup of shredded Cheddar or Cheddar Jack on one side from the middle to almost the edge. You can add a few chopped chiles if you choose. Fold the tortilla over the cheese. In a skillet, heat enough butter to cover the bottom, then put the folded tortilla into the pan and cook until lightly browned and cheese is mostly melted. Turn to the other side and cook it until browned.

About Albondigas

In Spanish, the word *albondigas* means meatball, as you might have deduced from the primary ingredient in this soup. However, you might not know that word origin is Arabic. It comes from al-bunduq, which translates to hazelnut. Meatballs are of a similar size and shape to a hazelnut, so they were likened to them and became the Spanish term for meatballs.

Often, rice is added to the meatballs as they are made, which makes them a bit like porcupine balls. To stay low carb but add a little more to the meatballs, you can add in 1/2 cup of riced cauliflower. This adds very little, about 0.2 carbs per serving, to your overall carb count. Alternately, you can just stir the cauliflower into the soup.

Apple Waffle Churros

These are a cheat as they only create the taste of a churro. Real churros are fried batter; whereas, this waffle goes for the seasonings to make it taste like a churro.

Waffles:
3/4 cups Low Carb Flour
1/4 cup Vanilla Whey Powder
1/3 cup Heavy Cream plus water to make 3/4 cup
3 tablespoons Butter, melted
1/2 tablespoon Baking Powder
1 Egg
1 tablespoon Sugar Substitute
1 teaspoon Cinnamon
1/2 teaspoon Vanilla

Churro topping:
1 cup Apples, diced
1 tablespoon Sugar Substitute
1/4 cup Butter
2 teaspoons ground Cinnamon
1/4 cup Pecans, chopped

Preheat the waffle iron while you mix the batter.

In a medium bowl, add the flour, whey powder, baking powder, and sugar substitute. If you aren't using whey powder, add 1/4 cup more of the low carb flour or almond flour. In a small bowl, mix the egg, cream, and vanilla together, then stir in the butter. Pour the egg mixture into the flour mixture and stir together until the batter is blended. If the batter is too thick to spread easily, add a little water.

Spray the waffle iron and pour about 1/2 cup of batter into the middle of the iron. Use a spoon back to spread it into each section. Close the iron, flip it if you have the option, then let it cook for about 2-1/2 minutes. The lid should lift easily when it is done.

Make the apple topping in a small skillet. Melt the butter over medium heat, then add the apple pieces, sugar substitute, cinnamon, and chopped pecans. Sauté them until the apples are fork-tender.

Separate the waffle into quarters and cook your second waffle. Put a quarter of the waffle on a serving plate, top with the apple mixture, add a dollop of whipped cream or whipped topping to it, then serve. Delicious. Makes eight servings.

Nutrition Information per serving:
 Calories: 180.6 Fat: 17.0 g Net Carbs: 5.0 g Protein: 6.1 g

About Churros

An actual churro is not a waffle, but sweet bread that is usually pressed through a pastry bag with a star tip to give it a ridge. It is then fried and covered with cinnamon and sugar. Possibly it originated in Spain when sheepherders made them as an easy breakfast they could cook over a fire. Or they may have come to Europe from China. Their origin is unsure. However, many cultures have fried bread and adding sweet to it is just a natural step.

The only thing that makes this waffle similar to a churro is that it has cinnamon and sugar in it, and you add more with the topping. But it makes a passable substitute for the real deal.

Beef and Zucchini Red Enchiladas

One of my original recipes, this creates the taste of a traditional enchilada using substitute ingredients.

1 pound Ground Beef
10 ounces Red Enchilada Sauce
2 cups Sharp Cheddar Cheese, shredded
4 Taco-size Whole Wheat Low Carb Tortillas
1/2 cup Onions, chopped
1/2 cup canned Green Chili Peppers, chopped
1 tablespoon Red Chili Powder
1 cup Zucchini, sliced 1/4 inch thick
1 tablespoon Olive Oil

In a skillet, add olive oil and heat. Add garlic and onions; cook until onion is just tender. Remove to a bowl. Add ground beef and cook, breaking into small pieces, until it is lightly browned. Drain any liquid off. Add 1/8 cup enchilada sauce and stir to mix. Add onions back to the pan and stir in green chiles.

Assemble the layers in a deep 9-inch round casserole dish beginning with 1/8 cup of enchilada sauce. Place a tortilla on top, then spread another 1/4 cup of sauce on top, then 1/3 of the meat mixture over the top of that. Arrange zucchini slices in a circle then top with 1/2 cup of cheddar cheese.

Place another tortilla on top of that, top with 1/4 cup sauce, then meat mixture, remaining zucchini slices distributed evenly around the outer circle, and top with 1/2 cup cheddar cheese. Place another tortilla on top and repeat with 1/4 cup sauce, the remaining meat, and 1/2 cup cheese. Top with a tortilla, spread remaining sauce over the top, and sprinkle cheese over it.

Bake in 350 degrees (F) oven for 25 to 30 minutes until the cheese is melted and casserole is bubbly. Cut into six slices. Top each serving with a fried egg if you would like. Serve Mexican Style Cauli-Rice as a side dish.

Nutrition Information per serving:
Calories: 516 Fat: 39.8 g Net Carbs: 8 g Protein: 31.3 g

About Enchiladas

The first mention of an enchilada came from the Mayan culture in the Yucatan Penisula. They made corn tortillas, called *tlaxcallin* in Mayan, which they filled with fish and rolled up to eat. The conquering Spanish called it a tortilla, which in Spain is actually more like an omelet. Over the years, the enchilada became a standard dish of Mexico with many fillings and sauces.

This recipe is made with low carb whole-wheat flour tortillas, which are not usually used to make enchiladas, but I haven't found a good low carb corn tortilla. Otherwise, it is a mostly traditional recipe.

Chile Verde

(Green Chile Pork Stew)

Chile Verde has been a staple in my life from childhood on. It is basically a green chile stew. In its purest form, it doesn't have red tomatoes in it, so I am always suspicious when a Mexican restaurant serves me the dish with red stuff in it. This makes a Texas authentic version of the recipe.

3 1/2 pounds Pork Butt or Shoulder, trim fat and cut into 2-inch cubes
2 teaspoons Salt
1 teaspoon freshly ground Black Pepper
1/4 cup Olive Oil
1 cup chopped Onions
1 4 oz. can chopped Green Chiles
1 to 2 Jalapeno Peppers, seeds removed, chopped
3 Garlic cloves, peeled and minced
2 12-oz. cans Tomatillos, drained
1 tablespoon dried Oregano
2 teaspoons ground Cumin
2 tablespoons ground Coriander
1 bunch Cilantro, chopped
3 cups Chicken Stock

Season the pork with salt and pepper. In a heavy pot, heat oil over medium-high heat and brown the pork cubes in batches. Turn to make sure all sides are browned. Remove the pork with a slotted spoon and put in a bowl. Repeat with each batch.

Pour off excess fat, then add peppers and onions to the skillet and cook over medium heat, stirring now and then until they are tender, about five minutes. Add the canned chiles and garlic, and cook a few more minutes.

Add the pork cubes, tomatillos, dried herbs, and cilantro, cover with chicken stock and bring to a boil then reduce to a simmer. With a wooden spoon, break tomatillos into smaller pieces as the stew cooks. Cook uncovered for 2-3 hours until the pork is fork-tender.

Adjust the seasoning to taste with salt and pepper. Makes twelve servings.

Nutrition Information per serving:
Calories: 486 Fat: 36.9 g Net Carbs: 3.8 g Protein: 32.0 g

About Chile Verde

Simply put, chile verde means green chile. Traditionally, it is made with pork, but you can also use chicken, lamb, beef, or a combination. The recipe varies quite a bit throughout Mexico and the Southwest. The version I adapted for this cookbook is a Tex-Mex version from West Texas. The key ingredient in any of these chili stews is the roasted green peppers, and those also vary depending on where you live and which variety is prevalent.

I use canned chiles in this recipe as they are roasted, peeled, and ready to go, but you can certainly start from scratch and roast your own peppers for it.

Chicken Tortilla Soup

  This recipe may look a little daunting with a long ingredient list, but it comes together quickly and easily, and it tastes delicious. To keep the carbs below 10 effective (or net carbs) per serving, I've cut back on the stewed or crushed tomatoes and red enchilada sauce. Be sure to check the cans for the lowest net carb count you can find on these. In place of regular corn, I've used baby corn, which is much lower in carbohydrates.

Cauliflower steps in for rice in the dish and adds more bulk to the soup. With the Mexican seasonings, this is a fabulous-tasting soup.

1/2 cup Onion, chopped
3 cloves Garlic, minced
1 tablespoon Olive Oil
2 teaspoons Chili Powder
1 teaspoon dried Oregano
1 teaspoon Cumin
1/2 can Crushed Tomatoes
1 cup Red Enchilada Sauce, canned
20 ounces Chicken Broth
1 tablespoon Better Than Bullion Chicken
1 cup Water
1/2 cup Dynasty Baby Corn, chopped
1 cup chopped or riced Cauliflower
1 (4-ounce) can chopped Green Chile Peppers
1/4 cup chopped fresh Cilantro
2 boneless half Chicken Breast, diced

Garnishes:
1 sliced Avocado for garnish
1/2 cup shredded Jack Cheese
Queso Fresco
1/4 cup chopped Green Onions
2 low carb Flour Tortillas, baked and cut into strips

Using a medium-sized stockpot, heat oil over medium heat. Add the onion and garlic, and sauté until they are limp. Stir in chili powder, oregano, and cumin along with the tomatoes, enchilada sauce, broth, bullion, and water. Bring to a boil then lower the heat to simmer for 10 minutes.

Add the chopped baby corn, chopped cauliflower, and chopped green peppers. Simmer for another 15 minutes to cook the cauliflower.

While it cooks, put tortillas on a foil-covered pan and bake in the oven or a toaster oven until they are lightly toasted and crisp. Cut into strips or break into pieces if you like.

Serve about one cup of soup in bowls and top with tortilla strips, avocado slices, Jack cheese, and chopped green onion, as you prefer. Sprinkle with Queso Fresco to top it off. Makes about eight servings.

Nutrition Information per serving:
Calories: 160 Fat: 9.3 g Net Carbs: 8.6 g Protein: 8.

About Queso Fresco

This Mexican cheese originated in Spain, where it was known as Queso Blanco. It is a mild farmers-type cheese made from cow's milk or a combination of cow's milk and goat's milk. While it is easy to make, it needs to be used or refrigerated soon after it is made.

Commercially made Queso Fresco or Queso Blanco keeps for a couple of weeks in the refrigerator. It is an excellent cheese for topping off the spicy Mexican dishes.

Irene's Baked Rellenos

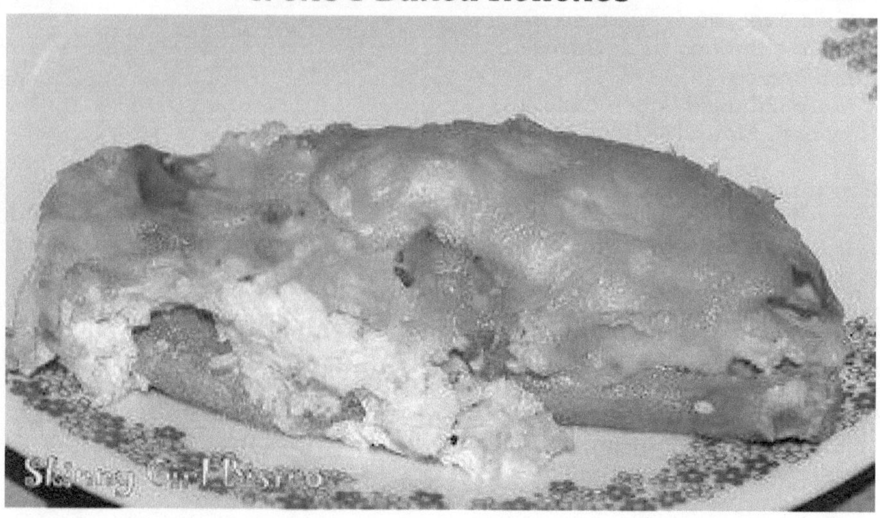

A simple to make casserole that combines the best of dipped and fried chile Rellenos with the ease of the canned chopped chiles version. It uses canned whole chiles that you stuff with cheddar or cheddar Jack cheese and chicken, then pour the batter over the top and bake them. Easy and delicious. If you prefer a vegetarian version, omit the chicken.

1 16-ounce can fire-roasted whole Green Chiles (8)
1 cup Fire-roasted Diced Tomatoes, Mexican style or add onions and
      peppers, if desired
8 ounces Chicken Breast, diced or shredded
4 ounces Cheddar Cheese, cut into 1/4 inch sticks
1 cup Shredded Mexican Four Cheese blend
4 Eggs
1/2 teaspoon Cayenne Pepper
1/4 teaspoon Salt
1/4 teaspoon Mexican Oregano
1/2 cup Heavy Whipping Cream
1/4 cup Water

Sauce Add-ins:
1/2 cup Onions, chopped
1/4 cup Peppers, sweet, red, raw, sliced

Preheat oven to 400 degrees F. Grease a 9x13-inch baking dish.

Split the chiles open, remove any seeds and spines, then stuff each with chicken and a stick of cheese. (The cheese should be about the length of the chile.)

Peppers stuffed with chicken and sliced cheese and the baked casserole.

In a bowl, add eggs, cream, and spices with 1/4 cup water and whisk together until well blended or put in your blender to mix. Pour the mixture over the chiles and cheese. Top with shredded Mexican cheese blend.

Bake in the preheated oven until set, about 40 minutes, then remove the casserole. Cover with foil to keep warm and let it rest for 10 minutes. It will set up and be easier to serve.

While the casserole sets, heat diced tomatoes in a saucepan. If you wish to add onions and peppers to the sauce, sauté them in a pan with a teaspoon of olive oil, then add to the tomatoes. Heat about 10 minutes on medium heat until hot.

Serve one chile topped with diced tomatoes and a salad on the side to make a light meal. Really hungry? Two chiles are only 11.4 g of net carbs with the onion and pepper add-ins in the sauce.

Nutrition Information per relleno without add-ins:
Calories: 236.4 Fat: 17.6 g Net Carbs: 4.0 g Protein: 14.2 g

Nutrition Information per relleno with toppings:
Calories: 264.4 Fat: 17.6 g Net Carbs: 5.7 g Protein: 14.5 g

Chile Cheese Cornbread Muffins

Once again, by substituting lower carb'd ingredients, you can have bread that tastes quite a bit like cornbread and has the same texture. I use a little cornmeal to give a bit of the flavor; however, flax meal serves as a good substitute.

3/4 cup Low Carb Flour
1 tablespoon Cornmeal
2 tablespoons Flax Meal
1 teaspoon Baking Powder
1 tablespoon Sugar Substitute
1/4 teaspoon Salt
1 large Egg
1/4 cup Cream
2 tablespoons Water
2 tablespoon melted Butter
1/4 cup chopped Chiles (Jalapenos, if you dare)

Preheat oven to 350 degrees (F). Prepare a muffin tin with cooking spray or line with paper cups.

In a bowl, combine the flour, cornmeal, and flax meal with sugar and baking powder and mix together. In a smaller bowl, beat the eggs, milk, and melted butter. Add the peppers and stir well.

Pour the egg mixture into the flour mixture and stir together until blended. Put an equal amount of batter in each of the cups, about 2 tablespoons in each one. The batter should come about 1/2 way up the muffin cup.

Bake for 30 minutes or until lightly browned. Serve warm with butter and sugar-free honey. Makes six muffins.

Nutrition information per muffin:
 Calories:150 Fat: 12 g Net Carbs: 2.1 g Protein: 6.6 g

About Cornbread

Corn was a prevalent New World crop, and the Native Americans had been cultivating it for a long time before the immigrants settled in New England. They made cornbread from their ground corn and shared their knowledge with the new arrivals. A quick bread, it only needs the corn to rise, so it gained popularity with the newcomers.

Various corns across the country resulted in several variations on cornbreads, from the yellow corn in the east to the blue corn in the south and the white corn in the west. It became a staple of the southern states.

My cornbread uses very little cornmeal in it since it is a high carb vegetable. When combined with the flax meal, it gives a flavor and texture profile similar to cornbread.

Mexican Chocolate Flan

2/3 cup granulated Sugar Alcohol*
3 ounces Hershey's Sugar-free Dark Chocolate
1 cup Heavy Cream
1/2 cup Cold Water
1 Cinnamon Stick or 1 teaspoon Ground Cinnamon
3 large Eggs
1/2 teaspoon Espresso Coffee Crystals
1/2 teaspoon Vanilla Extract
1/4 teaspoon Almond Extract

** This can be Xilytol or one of the other granulated sugar substitutes. Powder-based sweeteners do not caramelize well.*

You can also use 1/4 cup Sugar-free Caramel Syrup in place of making a sugar caramel. If you use this, use only 1/3 cup Sugar Substitute. I have also used sugar-free Maple Syrup.

To make the caramel, put the sugar alcohol crystals in a heavy pan and add 3 tablespoons water. Stir to dissolve, using a rubber spatula to remove any crystals from the side of the pan and push into the mixture. Cook until the mixture thickens and turns a golden brown. Put about 1 tablespoon in each of four ramekins. Place the ramekins in a deep pan or roaster.

Preheat the oven to 325 degrees (F.).

Chop the chocolate in a food processor to a coarse chop. In a
saucepan, add the rest of the sugar substitute (1/3 cup), the
heavy cream, cold water, chocolate, coffee, vanilla, and almond.
Cook over medium heat until the chocolate is completely melted
and the cream is just starting to bubble. Remove from the heat
and let cool down for a few minutes.

Put the eggs in a medium-sized bowl and beat until they are
thoroughly mixed. Add about 2 or 3 tablespoons of the chocolate
mixture and stir into the eggs, then add about 1/3 cup more and
mix it in and repeat until all the chocolate cream has been added
to the eggs. Do NOT add all at once as it might cook the eggs
instead of blending into them.

Use a 1/2 cup measure to divide the mixture into the four
ramekins. Carefully pour warm water into the pan holding the
ramekins until it is about 2/3 of the way up the side. Place the
pan in the middle of the oven and bake for about one hour until
a toothpick inserted in the center of the flan comes out mostly
clean, and it looks set. Remove to a counter to cool for about 30
minutes, then cover each ramekin with plastic wrap and
refrigerate for at least 2 to 3 hours before serving.

To serve, run a thin-bladed knife around the edge of the
ramekin, put a serving plate on top, and flip it over. Tap the
bottom of the ramekin a few times, and it should release. If it
doesn't release, use the knife to carefully slide under the flan
and push up gently on the bottom to break the tension seal, then
try again. Serve with a dollop of whipped cream, if desired.
Makes four servings.

Nutrition Information per serving:
Calories: 348 Fat: 32.1 g Net Carbs: 2.2 g Protein: 7.0 g

About Mexican Chocolate:

Cacao beans come from South America,
where the early Mayan civilization drank a
beverage they made from the dry roasted
beans, which were then shelled, and made into
a paste. When the Aztecs conquered the
territory, the beans had to be paid as tribute to
them. The cacao made its way to Spain via the
Conquistadors. Astorga, Spain, became the
European center for chocolate.

You can often find round cakes of
Mexican chocolate in grocery stores that carry
Mexican ingredients. It melts in hot milk. If

you add cinnamon and sugar or other sweeteners, it makes a delicious drink that is different from American chocolate, not as sweet and with a spicy taste.

Nopalitos Con Huevos

Nopalitos are the paddles of the Nopales cactus. These are available in stores that handle Mexican products, as well as in many regular markets in the southwest. I'm not sure about availability in other parts of the US or the world. I have a cactus in my yard, so it is close if I want one, but my local WinCo market usually has them in the spring and summer. The cactus is beneficial to your health and has a pleasant, fresh taste that goes well in this recipe.

1 young Nopales Paddle, cleaned, trimmed, and cut into strips
1/2 cup Pico de Gallo
1 Serrano Pepper, chopped
4 large Eggs
1 teaspoon Mexican Oregano
1 teaspoon Chile Powder
1/2 cup Chorizo Sausage
1/2 cup shredded Cheddar Jack Cheese
1/4 cup Queso Fresco
4 Low Carb Tortillas, 7-inch

Cook strips of nopalitos in water with 1/2 teaspoon salt and 1/2 teaspoon oregano. Drain when they are tender.

In a skillet, heat one-tablespoon oil, then add the nopalitos for a few minutes. Add the Pico de Gallo, Mexican oregano, and Serrano peppers. Continue to cook until the onions are almost done. Remove to a bowl.
Add a little olive oil to the pan, then add chorizo sausage and stir-fry until it is lightly cooked. Add the vegetables back to the pan and add chile powder.

Beat eggs in a bowl; add a bit of salt, pepper, and a little more oregano. Stir egg into the meat and vegetables, continuing to stir as they cook.

Sprinkle cheddar jack cheese over the top and remove from the heat.
Warm tortillas over the burner or in the oven. Serve eggs and sprinkle a little Queso Fresco over the top.

Serve with tortillas. Makes four servings.

Nutrition Information per serving:
Calories: 339 Fat: 24.1 g Net Carbs: 6.9 g Protein: 23.3 g

About Napalitos

While the Nopales cactus, which is also called a prickly pear cactus, is native to Mexico, it has spread around the world. Conquistadors took the plant back to Spain, where it spread to Africa and the Mediterranean area. The paddles are best when trimmed and grilled or boiled, but do not overcook, as they tend to get slimy.

This recipe combines them with eggs, which adds a fresh, clean taste to the meal, but they can also be used in stews, as a snack, and in many other ways.

Tex-Mex Beef Chile

I couldn't write a Mexican cookbook without including this recipe for Tex-Mex Chile. This is like my grandma made at home when I was growing up. It's a spicy, all-meat chile, not a bean in sight, which makes it a low-carb chile also. Delicious, but be cautious with the seasoning if you don't handle the heat too well.

2 pounds Beef Stew Meat
1/2 cup Low Carb Flour
1 large Onion. chopped
4-ounce can chopped Green Chiles
1 tablespoon Chili Powder
1 tablespoon minced Garlic
2 cups Stewed Tomatoes
1 teaspoon Seasoning Salt
1 cup Beef Stock
3 tablespoons Oil
Additional salt and pepper to taste
Shredded Cheddar Cheese for topping

Cut stew meat into bite-sized pieces. Heat oil in a cast iron or heavy stewing pot. Dredge meat in flour then put into stewing pot and lightly brown. Excess flour will fall off the meat into the pot, and that is ok. Remove the meat to a plate, then add more oil if needed. Add the garlic and onions. Cook until the onions are just tender.

Add beef stock, seasonings, stewed tomatoes, and chopped chiles. Mix well and add the beef back to the pot. Stir it up, bring to a boil, then lower the heat to a simmer, and cover the pot. Let it stew for about 2 hours, occasionally stirring until the meat is tender and the broth is thickened.

Serve in a bowl, top with shredded cheddar cheese and sour cream, if desired, and warm tortillas. (There are several brands of low carb flour tortillas available at the market.)

Makes six servings.

Nutrition Information per serving:
Calories: 243.2 Fat: 6.3 g Net Carbs: 7.6 g Protein: 36.3 g

About Tex-Mex Cooking

When I was growing up in Texas, I had never heard the term used to identify the food that was so prevalent in my home state. It actually describes the food that is a combination of Mexican cooking and Native American cooking.

The term was first applied to people who were of Mexican and Texan heritage or the Tejanos, which was the Spanish name for Texas. While many dishes were created in Texas that varied from Mexican food, the term wasn't applied to the cuisine until the 1970s when cookbook author Diana Kennedy made the distinction. Disdainfully, she pointed out that it wasn't "authentic" Mexican cooking and dismissed the Tex-Mex food. So, the chili with meat and beans, enchiladas, tacos, fajitas, and nachos that are the hallmark of Tex-Mex gained recognition in an unintended way. Another Tex-Mex innovation was the combination plate that put the rice and beans on the plate with the entrée.

Green Chile Chicken Skillet Casserole

A simple dish that is quick to make and delicious. It uses canned green enchilada sauce, canned green chiles, pre-made pico de gallo, and tasty vegetables to make a low carb and satisfying Mexican style meal. For variety, this same recipe works with shrimp or pork.

6 ounces Chicken Breast
4 tablespoons Pico de Gallo
1/2 cup Green Chile Enchilada Sauce
2 tablespoons Chopped Green Chiles
1 teaspoon Better than Bullion chicken plus 1/2 cup water
    or 1/2 cup chicken broth
1 cup Cauliflower, frozen or fresh, riced
1 cup Zucchini sliced or chopped
2 tablespoons Sour Cream
1/4 cup Cheddar Cheese, shredded
1 tablespoon Olive Oil

Chicken strips work well with this dish.

If starting with fresh cauliflower, parboil for 3 minutes and drain. If using frozen cauliflower, thaw and cook in the microwave for 2 minutes or parboil for 2 minutes, then drain excess water off. Process in a food processor for a few seconds until it is riced. Or you can chop finely or grate.

Cut the chicken into bite-sized cubes. Heat oil in a medium skillet and add the pico de gallo. Sauté about three minutes over medium heat. Move to one side and add the chicken to it. Cook until brown on both sides, then add chicken broth or bullion and water to the skillet along with the enchilada sauce. Stir in the chicken pieces and let come to a boil. Lower the heat to a simmer, then add the riced cauliflower and zucchini.

Cook for about 15 minutes until most of the liquid is reduced, and zucchini is fork-tender. Add the sour cream and cheese and stir in to mix well, cooking for about three minutes more to melt the cheese.

Serves 2 or 3 people, depending on how hungry you are.

Nutrition Information per servings (based on two servings) Calories: 274 Fat: 13.8 g Net Carbs: 5.7 g Protein: 26.2 g

Nacho Substitution

If you grew up in the Southwest United States, chances are you are a fan of nachos. Typically, these are made with corn chips, but those tasty fried pieces of tortilla are just too high in carbohydrates to have in your regular food plan.

An easy substitution is to use chicharrones, also known as pork rinds, pig curls, and bacon curls. You can buy these at the grocery store already cooked and in bags. They are probably located close to the corn chips. I use freshly puffed ones by purchasing a bag of microwaveable ones and preparing them before I make the nachos. Be warned, they take over two minutes to puff and look like dry jerky squares until they are cooked.

To make the nachos, put the puffed rinds onto the plate and cover with cheddar or cheddar jack cheese, then microwave about 30 seconds to melt the cheese. Serve with salsa and/or guacamole on the side. They are about 4 net carbs per serving with the salsa included

Grandma's Tex-Mex Spanish Cauli-rice

This recipe is based on my grandmother's Tex-Mex recipe for
Spanish rice. The only rice in this is the "riced" cauliflower that
has been chopped in a food processor to rice-sized pieces to
make a lower carbohydrate dish. If you don't have a food
processor, you can also grate the cauliflower. What's surprising
is how much this dish tastes like Spanish rice. In fact, I like it
better, and it is much lower in carbohydrates.

3 cups Cauliflower, about one 12-ounce package frozen, thawed
and
    riced (or you can use fresh cauliflower florets, cooked in
boiling water
    for about five minutes, then riced)
1 15-ounce can diced Tomatoes
1/4 cup Bell Peppers, thinly sliced or chopped
1/2 cup Onions, chopped
1 tablespoon Chicken Bullion Paste or packet of chicken
flavoring
1/4 cup Water
1 teaspoon minced Garlic
1 teaspoon Chili Powder
1 teaspoon Seasoning Salt
1 tablespoon Olive Oil or Butter

In a large skillet, cast iron is best, sauté garlic and onion in a
tablespoon of olive oil or butter over medium heat. Add canned
tomatoes, 1/4 cup of water, and riced cauliflower. Stir well.

Add the chopped peppers and seasoning, then cover the pan and reduce the heat to a simmer. Let cook until the liquid is reduced, and the cauliflower is tender, between 25 and 30 minutes. Makes about six servings.

Nutrition Information per serving:
Calories: 44 Fat: 1 g Net Carbs: 4.1 Protein: 2.6 g

Chicken and Spanish Cauli-rice Casserole with Cheese

You can easily add pre-cooked, diced, or shredded chicken or raw, shelled shrimp to the dish while it is cooking to make it a one-dish skillet meal. Or you can brown a pound of ground beef and stir it into the skillet at the same time as the chopped pepper. Don't stop there. Add sliced sausage links to it and a little Cajun powder, and you have a Creole-style dish.

Spaghetti Squash Tamale Pie

Squash fills in for many things in cooking, and I found that spaghetti squash is surprisingly good as a substitute for tamale dough. The filling for this pie brings all the flavors you expect, and the squash works really well with it.

1 pound lean Ground Beef
1 packet Taco Seasoning
2 1/2 cups Spaghetti Squash, (about half a medium-sized one)
1/2 cup Onions, chopped
1/4 cup chopped Black Olives (optional)
1 cup Mexican Style Four Cheese Mix
1/4 cup Queso Fresco
1 can (15.5 oz) Diced Tomatoes
1 tablespoon Chili Powder
1 teaspoon Cajun Seasoning
1 large Egg

Preheat oven to 350 degrees F.

Cook the spaghetti squash, remove seeds and use about 1/2 for this recipe. Put the rest away for another dish. Set aside.

In a large skillet, add a tablespoon of olive oil and sauté the onions. Add the ground beef and use a spatula to break into small pieces while cooking. Add your favorite taco seasoning and mix well. When lightly browned, add the diced tomatoes, cauliflower, chili powder, and Cajun seasonings. Stir well and cook for about 10 minutes.

In a bowl, mix together the spaghetti squash, egg, and half the cheese. Add a bit of salt, pepper, and a little Cajun seasoning.

Spray a baking pan or deep-dish pie pan with cooking spray and spread the spaghetti squash into it, smoothing it to form the crust and go up the sides of the pan. Fill this shell with the meat mixture. Sprinkle the remaining shredded cheese over the top and break the Queso Fresco into crumbles over that.

Spaghetti squash crust with filling in it.

Bake for about 30 minutes until the cheese is melted and lightly browned. Let cool for about 10 minutes then serve.

Makes six servings.

Nutrition Information per serving:
 Calories: 345.4 Fat: 23.6 g Net carbs: 8.7 g Protein: 21.3 g

Chicken & Chorizo Pizza

Using cornmeal and flax meal in this pizza crust hints at the texture and taste of a corn tortilla for a Mexican pizza. I used Basque chorizo for the sausage along with chicken that I bought grilled from the store. The green enchilada sauce adds a lighter chili flavor to the sauce.

Pizza Crust::
1 cup Low Carb Flour
2 tablespoon Cornmeal
2 tablespoons Golden Flax Meal
1/2 teaspoon Baking Powder
1/2 teaspoon Taco Seasoning
1/4 cup Water

Topping
1 cup cooked Chicken, white or dark meat, cubed or shredded
1 cup Basque Chorizo, ground or sliced
1 teaspoon Taco Seasoning
1/4 cup Jalapeno Peppers, chopped
6 Cherry Tomatoes, cut in half
1 cup Green Enchilada Sauce
1/4 cup Heavy Cream
1-1/2 cup Cheddar Jack Cheese

Preheat oven to 375 degrees (F.) Use a pizza stone or a baking pan. Spray with cooking spray or cut parchment paper to fit the pan.

In a medium bowl, mix the ingredients for the dough together. It should be thick and somewhat elastic. Turn onto a lightly floured (with low carb flour) breadboard and knead the dough until it isn't sticky. Roll or pat into an 8 to 10 inch round and transfer to the pizza pan. Bake in the oven for about 15 minutes until it is lightly browned.

In a skillet, cook the chorizo until just done. Mix with the chicken and add taco seasoning. Set aside. Clean out the skillet, then add the green enchilada sauce and the cream and mix together. Heat until just warm, then add 1/2 cup of the cheddar jack cheese. Spread the green sauce over the pizza crust, then top with the chicken chorizo mix, cherry tomatoes, and jalapenos.

Top with the cheddar jack cheese and bake in the oven for about 20 minutes until cheese is melted and lightly browned. Let cool about 10 minutes, then serve. A small salad or coleslaw completes the meal.

Makes four or six servings.

Nutritional information per serving (based on 4 servings):
 Calories: 369.6 Fat: 26.0 g Net Carbs: 9.5 g Protein: 21.9 g

Nutritional information per serving (based on 6 servings):
 Calories: 246.4 Fat: 17.3 g Net Carbs: 6.6 g Protein: 4.6 g

Tex-Mex Taco Pie

A quick-mix taco pie that has just a little cornmeal in the crust to give it that corn-tortilla taste without adding too many carbs. The cornmeal is optional. To make a lower carb version, omit the cornmeal and add 2 tablespoons of ground flax meal.

Many grocery stores carry pre-made Pico de Gallo and guacamole, so you can use those as time savers when serving this dish.

1/2 cup Low Carb Flour
1 tablespoon ground Golden Flax Meal
1 tablespoon Cornmeal
1 Egg
1/4 cup Heavy Cream
1/2 cup Water
1 teaspoon Red Chili Powder
1/2 teaspoon Garlic Powder
1/4 cup Onion, chopped
1/2 cup Cheddar Jack Cheese, shredded
1 cup Ground Beef, lightly browned
1/4 cup Mexican Chorizo
2 tablespoons Cilantro
1 cup chopped or torn Lettuce (Iceberg or Romaine)
4 tablespoon Pico de Gallo (onion, tomato, cilantro, and jalapeño chopped)
4 tablespoons Guacamole or 1/2 sliced Avocado

Heat oven to 425 degrees F. Spray a pie plate with cooking spray.

Combine the cream and water in a cup and mix. In a small bowl, mix flour, flax meal, cornmeal, egg, seasonings, and 1/2 the cream mixture. Stir well or beat with an eggbeater to remove lumps. Add the remaining cream and 1/2 the cheese and mix together. Pour into the pie pan. Bake for 20 minutes.

While the crust is baking, prepare the topping. In a skillet, lightly brown the ground beef. Don't let it get too cooked, just enough to brown it a little. Remove and drain on a paper towel.

Cook the chopped onions in the skillet until just softened. Remove to a paper towel with the meat. Put the chorizo in the pan and cook until it is melted and slightly cooked. Turn off heat. Add the ground beef, onions, and cilantro back to the pan and mix together.

Remove the pie pan from the oven and top with the meat mixture then sprinkle the remaining cheese over the top. Put back in the oven for another 15 minutes or until the cheese is lightly browned.

Cut into four slices and serve with lettuce, pico de gallo, and guacamole over the top or on the side.

Serves four.

Nutrition Information per serving:
 Calories: 376.2 Fat: 27.9 g Net Carbs 7.1 g Protein: 22.1 g

Without cornmeal (2 tablespoons flax meal)
 Calories: 380 Fat: 28.9 g Net Carbs: 4.3 g Protein: 22.6 g

15 Fabulous Recipes
Under 10 Net Carbs Each

Rene Averett

Author of Low Carb Recipe Magic Series

Breakfast Choices

for a Low Carb Lifestyle
Low-carb 15 Series

Rene Averett

Pepper Jack Florentine Omelet

2 large Eggs
2 pieces Thick Bacon, cooked and broken into pieces
1/4 cup Mushrooms, fresh, chopped
1/4 cup Spinach, fresh
1 tablespoon minced Onion
1Mini- Sweet Pepper, chopped
1 tablespoon Butter
2-3 tablespoons Pepper Jack Cheese, shredded
Salt & pepper to taste

In a small bowl, beat the eggs, minced onions, and seasonings together. Add a teaspoon of water.

In an omelet pan (6-inch skillet), heat 1 teaspoon butter to melting over medium heat, then add the mushrooms and sauté for about 2 minutes. Add the spinach and cook until it just wilts. Remove to a plate or paper towel. Add the rest of the butter to the pan, still on medium heat, then add the egg mixture. Cook, lifting the edges to let the mix run under the omelet as it sets until the top is only slightly moist.

If you like your omelet well done, then flip the omelet so the moist side will get brown also. To one side of the omelet, add the bacon, mushrooms, spinach, and most of the cheese, saving a little for the top. Fold the omelet over the fillings and sprinkle the rest of the cheese on top. Put a cover over the omelet for two to three minutes to help melt the cheese and finish the cooking. Turn off the heat and let it sit a minute, then transfer to your serving plate. Makes one omelet.

Nutrition information:
Calories: 390 Fat: 31.7 g Net Carbs: 3.1 g Protein: 19.8 g

Broccoli & Bacon Ricotta Quiche

I have made my quiches with ricotta cheese for many years, so this isn't an authentic quiche. It's a sturdy, filling variation that may become your preferred recipe also.

4 Eggs
1/4 cup Heavy Whipping Cream
1/2 cup Ricotta Cheese, whole milk
1/4 cup Mushrooms, fresh, sliced
1 cup Cheddar Cheese
1/2 cup Mozzarella Cheese
1 tablespoon Parmesan Cheese, grated
4 slices Bacon, fried and broken into pieces
2 tablespoons Onions, chopped
1/2 cup Broccoli, chopped & parboiled
Salt and Pepper to taste

Preheat oven to 350 degrees F. Use a cooking spray to lightly coat an 8x8" square pan or a deep-dish pie plate.

Bring a pan of water to a boil and add the broccoli. Cook for 3 minutes, then drain. Or put in a plastic wrap covered bowl in the microwave for 1 minute.

Mix together eggs, ricotta cheese, whipping cream, and seasonings. Reserve 1/4 cup of the cheddar jack cheese and mix the rest with the remaining ingredients into the eggs. In a skillet, melt 1 tablespoon butter over medium-high heat then add the onions and mushroom and sauté until just tender.

Put bacon, broccoli, and sautéed vegetables into the bottom of the prepared pan and spread evenly. Pour the egg and cheese mixture into the pan.

Bake for 40 to 45 minutes until eggs are set and lightly browned. Turn off the oven. Sprinkle the remaining 1/4 cup of cheese on top of the quiche and put back into the oven for another five minutes to allow the cheese to melt. Cut and serve.

Makes six servings.

Nutrition Information per serving:
Calories:218.5 Fat:16.5 g Net Carbs:1.9 g Protein: 15.0 g

This recipe is easy to adjust with various meats, vegetables, and cheeses. Swap in sausage or ham for the bacon, use asparagus instead of broccoli, and/or add a different cheese, such as Jack or Swiss.

Why is breakfast a big deal?

Often busy people get in the habit of skipping breakfast or just drinking coffee. There is a sound reason why you should eat something in the morning. When you're following a low carb lifestyle, your body is trained to expect fat to fire up the burners. If you think of your body as an engine that uses fat to run, then you get the idea that you need to prime your engine to begin running. The fat in your breakfast – butter, cheese, meat fats – provide enough to get the body started. Once it is running, you keep feeding it by eating something every couple of hours. The magic thing is that the fat burner will go to the fat stores in your body to get more to keep your energy going throughout the day. This is a simplified way of describing it, but it does work.

You may have read that if you starve your body while dieting, you will not lose weight. Science tells us that if you don't eat regularly, in small amounts, and give your body what it needs, it believes it is starving and stores the fats instead of burning them. I can personally attest to this as I have experienced it.

So no matter when your day starts, eat something for breakfast, even if it just an egg, a slice of cheese, or a couple of pieces of bacon.

Bacon and Avocado Omelet

Simple to make and a wonderful way to start your day. One of my favorites and it's only 3 net carbs. How can you beat that?

3 or 4 large Eggs
1/2 Haas Avocado, cut into slices
1/4 cup Cheddar Cheese
4 tablespoons Southwest Style Salsa (optional)
4 slices thick Bacon, broken into pieces
1 mini Sweet Pepper, clean and diced or sliced
Dash Pepper
1/4 teaspoon Seasoning Salt
1 tablespoon Butter

Break eggs into a bowl, add water, seasoning salt, and pepper. Beat until foamy. Heat a medium-size round bottom pan or omelet pan with 1 tablespoon butter over medium heat.

Add eggs and let cook for a couple of minutes until the egg sets on the bottom, then begin lifting the edges with the spatula and tilting the pan so that the uncooked egg runs underneath. Repeat, working your way around the pan. Keep lifting and tilting until most of the liquid egg is gone. This builds a fluffier omelet.

Evenly distribute the bacon and most of the cheese down one-half of the omelet. Use the spatula to lift and fold the omelet over the top. Reduce heat to low and put a lid over the pan. Let cook for about 3 minutes in order to melt the cheese.

Sprinkle 1 tablespoon of cheese over the top. Cut the omelet in half and serve each half with 2 tablespoons of salsa and half the avocado slices. If you wish, you can heat the salsa before serving. Makes two servings.

Nutrition Information per serving:
  Calories: 430 Fat: 35.3 g Net Carbs: 3.0 g Protein: 23.5 g

About Quiches and Omelets:

Whether or not the French actually conceived the omelet, they definitely gave it the name *omelette*. In its purest form, it is eggs whipped in a bowl with cream or water and chopped herbs, then cooked in a very hot omelet pan in a lot of clarified butter. Mod ern omelets are partially cooked, then filled with meats, vegetables, or whatever takes your fancy, then folded over to finish cooking and warm up the filling.

A *quiche*, also a French egg dish, is similar, but it is baked in a pie shell instead of cooking in a skillet. The name originated in the French province of Lorraine in 1605. However, other cultures used meat, eggs, and cream to make baked pies, so only the name is attributed to France.

Making a crustless quiche sets it back a step, but the flavor of the filling remains. Be adventurous with your omelets and quiches.

Bacon and Egg Skillet Scramble

So simple to do and so delicious. How can you go wrong with bacon? I used cottage-style bacon, which is similar to Irish and English bacon. It's a leaner cut than American bacon, but you can use regular thick-sliced bacon in it as well. Diced daikon radish fills in for potatoes, but you could also use diced turnips, cauliflower, or kohlrabi in it.

1 slice Cottage Bacon or 2 slices thick-sliced Bacon, broken into pieces
1 or 2 large Eggs
1/4 cup Daikon Radish, diced
1/4 cup Sharp Cheddar Cheese
2 tablespoons Pico de Gallo
1 tablespoons Butter
1/4 teaspoon Seasoning Salt

Precook the daikon in the microwave for 1 minute, add 1 tablespoon of butter to a small skillet and melt over medium heat. Add the daikon and cook for about 4 minutes, stirring it around, and turning it over.

Add the cooked bacon and mix together. Beat the eggs in a small bowl and add seasoning and a tablespoon of the cheese. Pour over the daikon and bacon, stir the eggs when they begin to set. Continue to cook until the eggs are almost done, stirring now and then. Distribute the Pico de Gallo on top, add the rest of the cheese, reduce heat to a simmer, and cover for about two minutes to melt the cheese. Makes one serving.

Nutrition Information:
  Calories: 433.5 Fat: 40.1 g Net Carbs: 2.1 g Protein: 15.0 g

Almond French Toast

Bread is always a nemesis in maintaining a low carb lifestyle. Fortunately, there are alternate choices for flour. This recipe uses almond flour or any low carb flour to make a simple microwave muffin as the base for French toast. This is a favorite recipe of mine and is so easy to do. You can make the muffin for this the night before or you can make up several and keep them in the refrigerator to use as needed. They will keep about a week.

For Magic Muffin:
1 tablespoon Almond Flour or other Low Carb Flour
1 tablespoon Vanilla Whey Protein Powder or Golden Flax Meal
1 Egg
1/4 teaspoon Cinnamon
1 tablespoon Coconut or other Oil
1 teaspoon Sugar Substitute

For Coating:
1 Egg
1/2 tablespoon Cream
1/4 teaspoon Cinnamon
1 tablespoon shaved Almonds
1 tablespoon Butter
1 teaspoon Sugar Substitute

Make the muffin first by mixing the egg and oil in a mug or a small even-sided bowl. Mix until the egg is thoroughly blended and it looks creamy. Add the almond flour, whey powder or flax meal, 1 teaspoon sugar substitute, and cinnamon and mix together until the flour is completely worked in. Microwave for one minute. Remove and use your fingertips to loosen the muffin in the bowl or mug. Let cool for a few minutes, then gently remove from the bowl/mug. Cut into two or three pieces across the middle to make rounds for dipping in the coating.

In a bowl or shallow pan, beat the egg until it is creamy yellow, then add the cinnamon, remaining sugar substitute, and cream. Mix together and put the slices of the muffin in it to soak about one minute on each side.

In a small non-stick skillet, heat the butter over medium-high heat until it is just bubbly. Add the almonds and stir with a spatula to lightly toast them, then put the coated muffin pieces into the pan and cook on top of the almonds. Cook about two minutes until the muffin is golden brown, then turn to the other side and cook another minute or two until it is done. Remove to a plate and serve with butter and sugar-free pancake syrup.

Makes one serving.

Nutrition Information per serving:
Calories:502 Fat: 2.1 g Net Carbs:2.9 g Protein: 22.0 g

Other Breakfast Options:

Granted that breakfast is an important meal, you might be wondering about other options than the ones in this booklet. For the most part, unless you have a high carb tolerance, cereals and bread are out of the picture.

The magic muffin used to make the French toast is a flexible bread made from low carb flour that can be microwaved or baked. Once cooked, it can also be sliced and toasted. See the Magic Muffin booklet for many ways to make this versatile bread.

You can also eat:
Ham slices
Bacon
Turkey slices
Roast Beef slices
White cheese slices
Hard-boiled eggs
1/2 cup mixed berries
1/2 cup cantaloupe
Low Carb breakfast bars
Low Carb drinks

Check out my blog for more breakfast ideas, like Breakfast Pizza. http://reneaverett.me/skinnygirl/

Pumpkin French Toast

 Based on my Baked French Toast recipe, this adds pumpkin and several spices to the flavor mix. The recipe is basically a bread pudding mix with a little less egg and cream. Top it with butter and sugar-free maple syrup.

2 slices of low carb bread or 2 Magic Muffins, toasted (see previous recipe)
1 large Egg
1 tablespoon Heavy Whipping Cream,
1 tablespoon Pumpkin Puree'
1 teaspoon ground Cinnamon
1/4 teaspoon ground Nutmeg
1 teaspoon ground Clove
2 tablespoons Pecans or Walnuts, chopped (optional)
1 teaspoon Vanilla Extract

Preheat oven to 350 degrees (F). Spray a 1-1/2 cup casserole dish with cooking spray or lightly butter.

Tear bread or muffins into small pieces and put them in a small mixing bowl. Add the rest of the ingredients and mix well to make a moist, lumpy batter. Pour into the casserole dish. Bake for 25 to 30 minutes until the pudding is done and a toothpick inserted in the middle comes out clean. Cut into two pieces. One piece is one serving.

Nutrition Information for one serving
 Calories:144 Fat: 12.6 g Net Carbs: 3.1 g Protein:4.4 g

I used New Hope Mills Blueberry Muffin bread mix to make a loaf of bread. It makes about 14 slices, and each slice is 2 net carbs. Two slices can be used to make the French toast casserole with or without pumpkin.

Curried Scrambled Eggs in Flatbread

My plan was to do curried eggs in a puff shell, but the batter with low carb flour simply refuses to puff up. It still tastes good, so I'm calling it a flatbread. You can, of course, eat the curried eggs without the bread option. This is a savory, tasty breakfast dish with a mild curry flavor, but you can adjust the spices as you like.

2 tablespoons Butter
1/2 cup Water
1/2 cup Low Carb Flour
1/8 teaspoon Salt
Pinch Pepper
Pinch dried Parsley, crushed
1 Egg

Preheat oven to 400 degrees (F.) Prepare three mini cake pans or 3 1-cup ramekins by spraying with Cooking spray.

In a small pan, add the water and butter and bring to a boil over medium-high heat. Add the flour and stir it vigorously to combine it with the butter and water. Continue to cook and stir until the mixture comes together into a ball and no longer separates. It will get fairly firm. Remove from the heat and let cool for 5 minutes.

Add the egg, and stir into the flour mixture. It will turn into a batter. Spoon the batter evenly into each of the prepared pans, about three tablespoons in each well.

Bake for 20 minutes, then check to see if they are golden brown. If not, bake another 5 minutes.

Remove from the oven and let cool a few minutes, then cut each one open and remove any uncooked dough in the middle. Let cool on a rack. These may be stored in the refrigerator in a plastic bag for a few days.

Makes three cakes.

Nutrition information per cake:
  Calories: 138 Fat: 12.3 g Net Carbs: 1.2 g Protein: 5.2 g

Curried Eggs

1/2 cup Ham cubes
2 to 3 Eggs
1 tablespoon Heavy Cream
1/2 teaspoon Curry Powder
1/4 teaspoon Red Pepper
1/4 cup Sweet Peppers, chopped
Pepper and Salt to taste
1 tablespoon Butter

Split two of the flat cakes in half. If the inside dough is not entirely done, put the halves under the broiler for about a minute. Or you can put them on a plate in the microwave for about 40 seconds to completely cook them.

In a small bowl, add the eggs, cream, and the seasonings and stir well to combine. If you like a strong curry flavor, add a little more curry powder.

In a non-stick skillet, melt the butter and add the ham cubes and chopped sweet peppers. Sauté about three minutes over medium heat. Add the eggs and stir with a wooden spoon, mixing the vegetables in, until the eggs are soft-cooked.

Remove from the heat and pile onto the bottoms of the bread. Top with the bread toppers and serve. You could add a little sugar-free orange marmalade on the side as a complement to the curry.

Makes two servings.

Nutrition information per serving:
  Calories: 238 Fat: 17.6 g Net Carbs: 2.2g Protein: 16.5 g

Total Net Carbs for combined eggs and bread dish: 3.4 g

Chorizo Eggs Rancheros with Guacamole

For a delicious Spanish-style breakfast, you can't beat Huevos Rancheros. The problem with ones at a restaurant lies mainly in the corn tortilla that forms the base. Even with a flour tortilla, the carbs are higher than you might want. Luckily, several companies are now making low-carb tortillas that come in at 3 net carbs per tortilla. I used Basque-style chorizo for this, which is firmer than the chili-oil saturated variety. A variation that uses a pancake for the base follows this recipe.

2 6-inch Low Carb Flour Tortillas
1 tablespoon Butter
1/4 cup prepared Guacamole
1/4 cup Salsa
2 large Eggs
4 ounces Chorizo
1/4 cup Cheddar Jack Cheese

Melt butter in a medium non-stick skillet and cook the tortillas, one at a time, lightly browning both sides. Set aside. Add chorizo to the skillet and cook, breaking apart with a spatula until browned. Stir in the salsa, 2 tablespoons of water, and cook for about four minutes until the liquid is reduced.

Remove chorizo and sauce to a bowl. Put 1/2 back into the skillet and bring to a bubble over medium heat. Make a well in the middle and break an egg into the center. Reduce heat to a simmer, cover with a lid and cook until a film forms over the egg yolk. Sprinkle 1 tablespoon of cheese over the top and cover for about one minute.

Spread 1 tablespoon cheese over a tortilla and put in the microwave for 15 seconds to melt the cheese. Spread half the guacamole over the tortilla, then slide the chorizo and egg mixture into the middle of the tortilla.

Repeat with the remaining chorizo and sauce. Makes two servings.

Nutrition information per serving:
Calories: 592.4 Fat: 49.5g Net Carbs: 6.8 g Protein: 29.1 g

Version 2

If you don't have access to low carb tortillas or if you just want a change, you can make this recipe using a Cornmeal and Flax Pancake that is still low carb although a little higher than the tortillas unless you make them very thin. You will notice that I served it a little differently with the guacamole and sour cream on the side as an option.

For this version:

Pancakes:
2 eggs
2 tablespoons Low Carb Flour
1 tablespoon Corn Meal
1 tablespoon Golden Flax Meal
1/4 teaspoon Taco Seasoning
1 tablespoon Oil
Pinch Salt
1/4 teaspoon Baking Powder
2 teaspoons Water

Topping:
1 tablespoon Butter
1/4 cup prepared Guacamole
1/4 cup Salsa
2 large Eggs

4 ounces Chorizo
1/4 cup Cheddar Jack Cheese

In a small bowl or container, add eggs and oil and use a small spatula to beat until the egg is blended into the oil and looks creamy. Add the rest of the ingredients and use the spatula to mix it together. Add enough water so that the batter is easily poured.

Heat a 6 or 7-inch non-stick skillet over medium-high heat and add 1/2 tablespoon butter. When the butter is melted and starting to sizzle, add 1/2 of the batter and swirl it around the pan to fill the space. Reduce the heat to medium. Cook until the sides set and bubbles begin to form. Put a lid over the pan and let cook another 30 seconds to partially bake the top. Turn the pancake over and cook for another 30 seconds to a minute until it is lightly browned.

Sprinkle a tablespoon of Cheddar Jack cheese on top of the pancake, then remove it to a plate and cover to keep warm. Repeat the process to make the second pancake.

Add chorizo to the skillet and cook, breaking apart with a spatula until browned. Stir in the salsa, 2 tablespoons water, and cook for about four minutes until the water is reduced.

Remove chorizo and sauce to a bowl. Put 1/2 back into the skillet and bring to a bubble over medium heat. Make a well in the middle and break an egg into the center. Reduce heat to a medium, cover with a lid and cook until a film forms over the egg yolk. Sprinkle 1 tablespoon of cheese over the top and cover again for about one minute.

Slide egg and chorizo on top of the pancake and add two tablespoons of guacamole or sliced avocados and sour cream, if desired, on the side.

Repeat with the remaining chorizo and sauce. Makes two servings.

Nutrition information per serving:
 Calories: 713 Fat: 58.9 g Net Carbs: 9.3 g Protein: 33.3 g

Note: You can cut the carbs to about the same as the tortilla version by using 2 tablespoons of golden flax and eliminating the cornmeal if you aren't that eager for the slight corn flavoring. You can also spread the batter in the pan very thinly, like making a crepe rather than making a thicker cake and make three or four pancakes instead of two.

Blueberry Dutch Puff Pancake

2 large Eggs
1/4 cup Whipping Cream
1/4 cup Water
1/4 teaspoon Vanilla Extract
2 tablespoons Sugar Substitute
1/4 teaspoon Salt
3 tablespoons Low Carb Flour
2 tablespoon Almond Flour
1 tablespoon Vanilla Whey Protein Powder
2 tablespoons Butter
1/2 cup Blueberries

Preheat oven to 425 degrees (F.)

Use an 8" cast iron skillet or an 8" heavy pie pan to bake this.

In a blender, add the eggs, whipping cream, water, vanilla extract, salt, and sugar substitute and blend for a few seconds. Add the low carb flour, almond flour, and protein powder and mix until the batter is smooth.

If you are using the pie pan, put it in the oven to get hot, then remove it and let the butter melt in the pan. If you're using the skillet, melt the butter in the skillet over high heat until the butter gets bubbly. Remove from the heat.

Spread the blueberries around the pan or skillet evenly. Pour the batter over the blueberries carefully. Put in the oven and bake for 18 to 20 minutes or until golden brown.

Let cool about 5 minutes, then cut into 4 wedges and serve with powdered sugar substitute over the top. These can also be a satisfying light dessert with a dollop of whipped cream on top. Makes four servings.

Nutrition Information per serving
Calories: 195 Fat: 16.7 g Net Carbs: 3.9 g Protein: 7.1 g

About Dutch Puff Pancakes:

Originating, probably, in Germany, this is a puffed popover-type pancake. Using about equal amounts of egg and milk or cream with flour, the batter is sometimes seasoned with vanilla and cinnamon. The first recipe I found in Betty Crocker's International Cookbook many years ago called it a German pancake. The name Dutch Baby came from an American restaurant that coined and copyrighted, the name. It is also called a Bismarck or a Dutch Puff.

Although the original recipe called for lemon, butter, and powdered sugar as a topping, syrup and fruit jam might also be served with it. The cookbook recipe I based this on incorporated sliced apples into it, which is another way it is made. I have made these with several varieties of fruit, and most work well in it. Apple is a little high for a low carb lifestyle, but if you use thin slices and space them out, you can work it in. Berries go well and are the lowest in carbs of the fruits.

Most low carb flours make a tasty pancake, but they do not puff into popovers, so they will not have as much puffiness.

Flourless Sweet Muffins

While I say "flourless," I refer to wheat flour, which is totally missing from this recipe. Instead, this uses a small amount of coconut flour, combined with cream cheese and eggs to get the almost sponge-cake-like texture. You can substitute almond extract for the vanilla to change up the flavor, or you could add 1 teaspoon cinnamon to give a spicier taste.

2 tablespoons Coconut Flour
2 oz. Cream Cheese
2 Eggs, separated
1 tablespoon Butter
1/4 cup Sugar Substitute
1 teaspoon Vanilla
1/4 teaspoon Cream of Tartar
2 tablespoons Water

Preheat oven to 315 degrees (F). Prepare a muffin tin by spraying with cooking spray or use 5 individual silicone muffin molds and spray them with cooking spray.

In a medium bowl, add the egg whites and cream of tartar. Beat with a mixer until stiff peaks form. Set aside. In a smaller bowl, add cream cheese, butter, and sugar and cream together. Add egg yolks, vanilla, water, and coconut flour. Mix together until completely combined. Fold the egg yolk mixture into the egg whites as carefully as possible so that it doesn't break down the whites. Continue to lift and fold the mixture until the egg yolk mixture is blended into the whites.

Spoon 2 tablespoons batter into each muffin mold. It will make 5 muffins. Bake for 18 minutes until just lightly browned. Remove and cool.

Nutrition Information per muffin:
 Calories: 116 Fat: 4.1 g Net Carbs: 2.0 g Protein: 3.4 g

Lemon Zucchini Bread

Adding zucchini to bread batter cuts the carbs while adding more flavor to make this delicious bread with a light lemon flavor. Great for breakfast or anytime. It also freezes well.

1-1/2 cups shredded Zucchini
3/4 cup Sugar Substitute
2 Eggs
1 Egg White
1/2 cup Vegetable Oil
1 cup Low Carb Flour
2 tablespoons Coconut Flour
1/4 cup Vanilla Whey Powder
1/4 teaspoon Salt
1/2 teaspoon Baking Soda
1/4 teaspoon Baking Powder
Zest of 1 Lemon
1 tablespoon Lemon Juice

Preheat oven to 350 degrees (F.) Prepare a small bread pan by spraying with baking spray or line with parchment paper on the bottom and spray the sides.

In a large bowl, mix the eggs, egg white, oil, and sugar substitute together and beat with a mixer until well blended. Stir in the lemon juice and lemon rind. Stir in the shredded zucchini.

In a separate bowl, mix the flours, whey powder, baking soda, and baking powder together. Add to the egg mixture in three or four small batches, stirring in well with each addition.

Pour the batter in the bread pan and spread to level it. Bake for 50 to 55 minutes until the center springs back when you press on it lightly or until a toothpick comes out clean. Makes 10 slices.

Nutrition Information per slice:
Calories: 169.3 Fat: 14.1 g Net Carbs: 2.7 g Protein: 6.6 g

About Vegetable or Fruit Breads:

While Zucchini Bread is often seen in recipe books, this basic recipe can be applied to many other bread loaves using vegetables and fruit. Shred whichever raw vegetable you are planning to use and measure the same amount in the recipe. Good choices for it are carrots, beets, butternut squash, or any summer squashes that are grated.

Fruits include grated apples or quince, diced or pureed persimmons, peaches, pears, or fresh berries. If you use cranberries, you need to add sugar. Most of the fruits are a little high for low carb, so they would need to be used sparingly in the recipe. I would suggest using about half the amount and adjusting the carb count accordingly.

Ricotta Applesauce Waffles

This is so good that I have it often. The ricotta cheese adds lift to the waffles while the applesauce adds flavor and moisture. I use a Belgian waffle iron to make these.

1/4 cup Low Carb Flour
2 tablespoons Vanilla Whey Protein Powder
1 tablespoon Almond Flour
1 large Egg
1 tablespoon Ricotta Cheese
2 tablespoons Unsweetened Applesauce
1 tablespoon Oil
1/2 teaspoon Ground Cinnamon
1/2 teaspoon Baking Powder
1 tablespoon Heavy Whipping Cream

Spray Belgian waffle iron with cooking spray. While iron heats, mix the batter.

In a small bowl or in a food processor, add egg and oil and mix together until thoroughly blended. Add applesauce and whipping cream and mix together. Then add the rest of the ingredients and mix until combined.

Pour the batter into the waffle iron, spreading it evenly into each section. Close the iron and cook for about 2-1/2 minutes until the steam from the waffle is almost gone. Carefully lift the lid. If the waffle is done, it will release easily. If there is resistance, let it cook a little longer. Cut waffle in two and serve. Makes two servings.

Nutrition Information per serving:
Calories: 248 Fat: 19 g Net Carbs: 4.3 g Protein: 14.2 g

Fast Food Style Breakfast Sandwich

A make-at-home favorite muffin, sausage, and egg breakfast sandwich made the low carb way. I have an electric sandwich maker that makes this easy to do. You can swap the sausage out for ham or bacon easily. I prefer my eggs scrambled, but you can make them sunny side up easily.

The first instructions are to make it without a sandwich maker. An egg ring helps to make round eggs, If you don't have an egg ring, you can cut the top and bottom out of a tuna can, using a pair of pliers to press down any rough edges on the rim.

Muffin:
1 Egg
1 tablespoon Oil
1 tablespoon Golden Flax Meal
2 tablespoons Low Carb Flour
Dash Ground Pepper
Pinch Salt
1 tablespoon grated Parmesan Romano Cheese

Filling:
1/4 lb. Ground Sausage or use a precooked patty
1 Egg
1 slice American Cheese
1 tablespoon Butter
1 tablespoon Mayonnaise (optional)

Mix all the ingredients for the muffin in a 3 1/2 to 4-inch microwavable bowl with straight sides. Be sure to beat the egg well so that there are no strings of white when the muffin cooks. Microwave for one minute and let cool for a few minutes. Rock the muffin with your fingertips to release it from the bowl. Cut the bread across the middle as you would an English muffin and butter.

Press the sausage into a 4-inch patty and cook in a skillet until done. Clean the pan out, then spray with cooking spray and heat over medium-high heat. Using an egg ring, spray the sides and put in the pan to heat. Break an egg into a small bowl or cup and add any seasonings you like, such as salt and pepper, then gently slide the egg into the ring. The pan needs to be hot, or the egg will run out under the ring. Cook until the egg sets, then remove the ring and flip the egg over.

Toast the muffin in a toaster or under the broiler. Put the slice of American cheese (or cheese of choice) on the bottom, then put under the broiler for about one minute to melt the cheese. Put the sausage on top, then the egg, and put the muffin top on it. Enjoy. Add mayonnaise or any other preferred condiment.

If you have a sandwich maker, this is even easier. Prepare the muffin and sausage as described. Heat the sandwich maker and spray with cooking spray. Put the muffin bottom into the bottom ring and put the sausage on top, then the cheese on top of that. Move the top section and center plate over the bottom well. Put the egg in the top section, pierce the yolk with a toothpick if you are making a sunny side up egg. Close the cover and cook for about two minutes, then put the muffin top into the top well and close again. Cook for two more minutes and serve. Makes one sandwich.

Nutrition Information per sandwich:
  Calories: 760 Fat: 66.8 g Net Carbs: 4.8 g Protein: 13.8 g

Asparagus & Bacon Frittata

A frittata is an open-faced omelet. Instead of folding and turning, you cover the eggs and fillings with a lid to finish cooking or put it in the oven for about 10 minutes.

2 Eggs
1/2 cup Asparagus, cut into pieces
2 slices thick-cut Bacon
1/2 cup Cheddar Cheese or White Cheese, shredded
1 tablespoon Heavy Cream
1 tablespoon Butter
Salt & Pepper to taste
1/4 teaspoon dried Basil, crushed

In a small bowl, break the eggs, add the cream and seasonings, and beat until mixed. Set aside. Cook bacon until it is crisp or to your preference.

In a 7" non-stick skillet, melt butter over medium-high heat. When the butter bubbles, stir the eggs and add to the skillet. Tilt the pan to spread the eggs all over the pan. Let cook, lifting the edges with a spatula to allow the uncooked eggs to run underneath a few times. When the edges are mostly set, add the asparagus and bacon, making sure to distribute evenly over the surface. Sprinkle the cheese over the top.

Cover the pan and lower the heat. Cook for about a minute or until the eggs on the top of the frittata are done, and the cheese is melted. Slide the frittata onto a plate and serve.

Makes one frittata that will serve one hungry person or two less hungry people. Add a side of fruit or a low carb muffin.

Nutrition Information per frittata:
 Calories:673.3 Fat: 55.8 g Net Carbs: 4.9 g Protein: 34.6 g

About Frittatas:

Similar to an omelet, the frittata may have originated in the Middle East or possibly in Italy. As it was considered a throw-together meal using leftovers, cooks in the Mediterranean may not have bothered with recipes. It is often considered the Italian open-faced omelet. From Spain, where it was called a tortilla, the frittata became a dish based on sliced potatoes along with the eggs.

Since it is great for using leftovers, you can put any combination of meat and vegetables in it to cook. You can use two or three eggs when making it, mix them up well, and pour them into a buttered or oiled skillet, preferably one that can go into the oven. A cast-iron skillet works well, although I have used a copper skillet that also is safe in the oven. You cook it partially on the stovetop, then transfer it to the oven at about 350 degrees to finish cooking.

Spicy Scotch Eggs

I love this variation on traditional Scotch Eggs. It combines chorizo sausage with regular pork sausage and replaces the breadcrumbs with seasoned almond flour. Delicious for breakfast or brunch. To make it easier, you can buy hard-boiled eggs at many grocery stores, so you don't have to cook and peel them, which is a time-saver.

4 medium or small hard boiled Eggs
1/2 lb Pork Sausage
1/2 lb Chorizo Sausage
1 Egg
1/4 cup Cheddar Jack Cheese
Salt & Pepper to preference
1/4 cup Almond Flour
1/4 teaspoon Seasoning Salt

Preheat the oven to 365 degrees (F.)

In a medium bowl, combine the pork sausage and the chorizo sausage. Use Basque-style chorizo that isn't mixed with chili sauce. Add the salt and pepper to your preference, then add the cheese and mix together well.

In a saucer, put the almond flour and add a little seasoning salt to it. Break the egg into a bowl and beat it until it is completely mixed with no white strings.

Prepare a baking sheet by covering with aluminum foil or parchment paper sprayed with baking spray or a non-stick silicone mat. Divide the sausage into quarters and roll into a ball. Press the ball flat, then fold it around the egg, sealing the edges together. Dip the sausage ball into the egg, then roll it in the almond flour. Set the coated egg on the baking sheet. Repeat with the rest of the eggs.

Bake for 30 to 40 minutes until the sausage is done. Makes four servings.

Nutrition Information per serving:
 Calories: 681 Fat: 53.1 g Net Carbs: 3.5 g Protein: 45.4

Pumpkin Cheese Cereal

When I first read this recipe, I was a little skeptical. However, I am willing to give most things a try. The original called for ricotta cheese, but I didn't have any, so I substituted cream cheese. I also added a couple of ingredients to bring more flavor, and this turned into a delightful, creamy pudding-like breakfast cereal, similar to cream of wheat.

If you like pumpkin, this is a real treat. One of my favorite breakfast options has always been leftover pumpkin pie. This tastes almost as good. If you want, you can make it without the pumpkin and use other seasonings or fresh berries. You can also put a tablespoon of sugar-free jam of your choice in it. Apricot, peach, orange marmalade, and strawberry work well. Another option is to stir in 1 or 2 tablespoons of sugar-free applesauce, peanut butter, or almond butter in place of the pumpkin.

The carb count for most add-ins will be close, but pears, peaches, apples, and other higher carb'd fruits will add to the count.

1/4 cup Ricotta Cheese, Small Curd Cottage Cheese, or Cream Cheese
1 Egg
3 tablespoons Pumpkin Puree'
1 to 2 tablespoons Sugar Substitute
1/2 teaspoon ground Cinnamon
1/8 teaspoon ground Cloves
2 tablespoons Golden Flax Meal or Almond Flour
1 tablespoon Butter
1/2 tablespoon Cream
1 pinch Salt
5 Pecan or Walnut halves, broken into pieces (optional)

If you are using cream cheese, measure it into a microwave-safe bowl and heat it for 15 seconds to soften. Add 2 tablespoons hot water and stir to mix the water into the cream cheese. It should be a runny liquid at this point. Add a little more water if needed. Stir in the egg, mixing very well so that the white is completely stirred into it.

Add pumpkin and seasonings at this point and stir them in.

In a non-stick skillet, add 1/2 the butter and melt over medium heat. Spread the butter around the skillet, then add the egg & pumpkin mixture. Stir as it cooks so that it doesn't form a pancake. You need to stir more vigorously than you do for scrambled eggs. As it begins to thicken, add the flax meal and nuts, if you are using them, and continue to stir until it is thick and looks done, about 30 to 40 seconds more.

Serve in a bowl with the rest of the butter and a little cream.

Nutrition Information:
 Calories: 358 Fat: 29.7 g Net Carbs: 4.5 g Protein: 14.3 g

Magic Muffins
for a Low Carb Lifestyle

15+ Fabulous Recipes
Under 10 Net Carbs Each

Rene Averett

Author of Low Carb Recipe Magic Series

Low Carb Magic Muffins
Low Carb 15 Series

Rene Averett

Basic Magic Muffin

My variation on the Muffin-in-a-Minute uses low-carb flours and additional ingredients to adapt it to make a variety of tasty muffins. When I say low-carb flour, it can be a Baking Mix, which is made by several companies that produce low-carb mixes, almond flour, soy flour, or any other nut flour. Coconut flour can be used, but it requires more liquid and needs to be adjusted. See next page.

1 Egg
1 tablespoon Oil (vegetable, coconut, or olive oil)
1 tablespoon Low-carb Baking Mix or Low-carb Flour
1 tablespoon Flax Meal, regular or golden
1 teaspoon Sugar Substitute
1/2 teaspoon ground Cinnamon
1/2 teaspoon Baking Powder
Pinch Salt

In a microwavable cup or bowl, mix the egg and oil together. Add the rest of the ingredients and mix well. Tap the cup a few times to get the air bubbles out. Put the cup in the microwave and cook it for one minute. Presto! A big fluffy and moist muffin is produced.

You can butter it and eat it as is or cut it into slices and toast it under a broiler. If you make it in a 3 1/2 inch bowl, you have a thick muffin that you can slice across the middle to make 2 slices big enough to go in a toaster. This tastes great when toasted. For muffins from a smaller container, butter and put under the broiler or in a toaster oven.

Nutrition Information for one muffin:
 Calories: 255 Fat: 22.8 g Net Carbs: 2.4 g Protein: 9.3 g

Coconut Flour Muffin

As I said, using coconut flour is a little different because it is very dry flour that expands when liquid is added. It is also higher in carbohydrates than the other nut flours. Therefore, you have to adjust the recipes to take this into consideration. All the lift in any baked goods made with coconut flour comes from eggs. Baked goods tend to be more delicate when you use alternate flours, such as coconut flour and nut flours, so it is important to let them cool before you try to move them. The other issue I find with coconut flour is that it tends to be gritty, but if you don't mind it, then it's a good substitute flour.

1 Egg
1 Egg White or 2 tablespoons Liquid Egg Whites
1 tablespoon Oil (vegetable, coconut, or olive oil)
2 tablespoon Coconut Flour
1 teaspoon Sugar Substitute
Water as needed
Pinch Salt

In a microwavable cup or bowl, mix the egg and oil together. Add the rest of the ingredients and mix well. Let rest for a couple of minutes. Coconut flour absorbs liquid, so add extra water until you have a thick, but still batter-like consistency. Tap the cup a few times to get the air bubbles out. Put the cup in the microwave and cook it for one minute. If it still looks too moist, like batter, cook it 15 seconds longer. Remove from microwave and let cool at least 5 minutes before removing the muffin from the cup. Use a serrated knife to slice the muffin if you cut it in half or thirds.

The muffin is tall and pale when it comes out of the cup.
Slice in half or into thirds.

Butter or top with low-carb jam and enjoy. You can also toast it before buttering. I butter my cup-sized slices and put them under a broiler at 450 degrees (F.) for about 5 minutes to toast. Keep a close eye on them so they don't burn. You can also put them in a toaster oven. For bowl-sized muffins, I slice across the middle and put them in a toaster.

Nutrition Information for one muffin:
 Calories: 257 Fat: 19.9 g Net Carbs: 3.4 g Protein: 9.4g

Note: Be sure to check the net carbs (carbohydrates minus fiber) on the coconut flour that you select. These vary depending on the manufacturer. Some are as low as 2 net carbs per tablespoon while others are up to 4 or 5 net carbs.

This is a very basic Coconut Muffin recipe. Add in cinnamon, vanilla, or berries to add to the flavor. For a savory flavor, add cheese, garlic, rosemary, dill, or other spices.

Cornmeal Magic Muffin

These can be cooked in the microwave or in the oven. The texture is different depending on how it is baked. Again, the microwave muffin can be cut and toasted, which also changes its texture and taste. So try it each way and pick your favorite. My picture shows baked ones.

1 large Egg
2 tablespoons Low-carb Flour
1 tablespoon Extra Virgin Olive Oil
1 tbsp Grated Parmesan Cheese
1/4 teaspoon Salt
1 tablespoon Golden Flax Seed Meal
1 teaspoon Corn Meal
1/2 teaspoon Sugar Substitute

In a small bowl, mix the egg and olive oil until well blended. Then stir in the rest of the ingredients until they are fully mixed. Can this be easier?

To microwave, put in a cup or a 3" in diameter bowl and cook in the microwave for 1 minute. Let cool a few minutes, cut and either butter and eat or toast, then butter and eat. Makes one muffin.

To cook in the oven, preheat the oven to 360 degrees (F.) Spray a muffin pan with cooking spray. Fill two muffin tins to 2/3 full (about 2 tablespoons each). Put a little water in any empty wells then cook for 18 to 20 minutes. Cool a few minutes, butter, and serve. Makes two muffins.

Nutrition Information per recipe:
Calories: 275 Fat: 22.1 g Net Carbs: 4.2 g Protein: 12.1 g

Flax Meal Muffin Buns

How much you like this muffin depends on how much you like flax meal. You can use either regular or golden flax meal in it. You can also vary the amount you use. If you don't like a complete flax muffin, then use half flax and half of another low-carb flour, such as almond flour. You can make this sweet or savory depending on what spices you use. It's not unusual for a muffin to have air bubbles. When you cut this one open, it resembles an English muffin with many little holes to fill with butter.

2-1/2 tablespoons Ground Flax Meal
1/4 teaspoon Baking Powder
Pinch Salt
1/2 teaspoon Sugar substitute
1 large Egg
1 tablespoons Olive Oil,
1/2 teaspoon ground Cinnamon OR 2 teaspoons grated Parmesan Cheese

In a microwavable bowl or cup, mix together the wet ingredients, then add the rest of the ingredients and mix well. Make sure the egg is completely mixed in.

Place in the microwave and cook on high for one minute. Let cool a few minutes, then cut and toast or just butter and eat. This is delicious with a thin coat of peanut butter on it.

Nutrition Information per muffin
  Calories: 270 Fat: 24g Net carbs: 1.0 g Protein: 10.1 g

Almond Chocolate Pudding Magic Muffin

The trick to making this into a rich chocolate muffin is to undercook it slightly so that it stays moist. Oh, and I add a little chocolate pudding mix and cream cheese to help add more flavor and texture. Decadent!

1/4 cup Egg whites
1 tablespoon Butter
1 oz. Cream Cheese, softened
3 tablespoons Almond Flour
2 teaspoons sugar-free Chocolate Pudding Mix
1 tablespoon Sugar Substitute
1/2 teaspoon Vanilla Extract
2 tablespoons Sugar-free Chocolate Chips

In a small bowl, mix the egg whites, butter, cream cheese, and pudding mix together until blended. Add the rest of the ingredients, except the chocolate chips, and mix well. The batter should be thick, but not dry. If it appears too dry, add a teaspoon of water and stir it in. Divide the batter into two 3/4-cup ramekins or small cups and gently stir in the chocolate chips.

Cook in the microwave for 1 minute, then let sit about 5 minutes to cool. Sprinkle a little powdered sugar substitute over the top and serve in the ramekin or cup or run a thin knife around the edge, lift the bottom to release any suction, then flip onto a serving plate. Makes two servings.

Nutrition Information per muffin:
Calories: 299.2 Fat: 26.3 g Net Carbs: 2.6 g Protein: 13.9 g

Flax Meal & Almond MM Ham and Cheese

Sometimes a simple recipe is one that you miss the most when you adopt a low-carb lifestyle. Many foods with high-fat content are okay, but other things that have the starches, like bread, potatoes, and the like, are off limits. So to be able to make a sandwich with a low-carb bread is almost a miracle. Most low-carb bread doesn't have the flavor of a wheat bread, but some of them taste pretty amazing on their own.

This delicious brunch sandwich starts with a Flax Meal Almond Flour Magic Muffin. Add cheese and ham and you have a comfort food breakfast or lunch. If you happen to have one of the sandwich makers, this sandwich can be cooked in that easily once you make the microwave muffin. Check the carb counts on the cheese and the ham that you buy to make this. They vary depending on who makes it and what it contains in additives. A honey ham is going to have carbohydrates in it while a plain ham has none. Some cheeses have quite a few carbs (American processed cheese is 2 net carbs per slice) while others may have 0 carbs.

1 large Egg
1 tablespoon Olive Oil
1 tablespoon Golden Flax Meal
1 tablespoon Almond Flour
1/2 teaspoon Sugar Substitute
1/4 teaspoon Garlic Herb Seasoning
Sprinkle Crushed Chile Peppers

In a 3 to 3-1/2 " microwaveable bowl, add the egg and oil and mix with a rubber/silicone spatula or whisk until the egg is completely blended. You do not want any egg white strings in the muffin. Add the rest of the ingredients and mix well. Thump the bowl on the counter a couple of times to try to reduce any air bubbles in the batter.

Microwave for 1 minute. Remove and let sit for about 5 minutes to cool down. This makes it easier to handle and cut. Use a serrated knife to cut across the middle to make two slices.

For the Filling:
2 slices American Cheese or Swiss Cheese
1 or 2 slices of thinly sliced Ham
Butter

Heat a heavy skillet - I used my copper clad skillet for this although a cast iron or other heavy one works - and add a tablespoon butter to melt over medium high heat. Butter the top and bottom of the muffin, then place the bottom in the hot pan and top with a slice of cheese, the ham, and the other slice of cheese. Put the muffin top over the top slice of cheese.

Cook the sandwich, pressing it on a little with a pancake spatula to seal the bread to the melting cheese. This takes a few minutes to begin melting the cheese. Turn it over and cook the other side. If the bread isn't browned yet or the cheese isn't melted, then flip it again after another three or four minutes. Cook until the cheese is melted and the bread is lightly browned.

Remove to a plate and serve. I like a little mayonnaise with mine, so I put about a teaspoonful on the side of the plate to dip the sandwich in as I eat.

Makes one sandwich.

Nutrition Information per sandwich (American Cheese - 2 net carbs per slice):
Calories: 616.6 Fat: 55.9 g Net Carbs: 5.8 g Protein: 20.5 g

Nutrition Information per sandwich (Swiss Cheese - 0 net carbs per slice):
Calories: 566.6 Fat: 53.9 g Net Carbs: 1.8 g Protein: 19.5 g

Savory Magic Muffin Toast

A nice side-toast to go with BBQ or Italian food where you might like a bread with complimentary seasonings in it, such as garlic and rosemary along with Parmesan cheese or perhaps some oregano or even dill in the bread. This is a variation on the Muffin-in-a-Minute that is microwaved, then toasted. It uses more low-carb flour to make a thick, tall muffin that can be cut in half and easily toasted. Use a one-cup ramekin, preferably about 3.5" to 4" wide so it pops up in the toaster easier.

2 tablespoons Low-carb Baking Mix
1 tablespoon Golden Flax Meal
2 teaspoons Parmesan Romano Grated Cheese
1/4 teaspoon Baking Powder
Pinch Sugar Substitute
1 large Egg
1 tablespoon Olive Oil or melted Butter
1 teaspoon Garlic Powder or 1/2 teaspoon minced garlic
1/2 teaspoon dried Rosemary, crushed (or other savory of your choice)
Pinch Salt

Spray a ramekin with baking spray. In a small container, mix all ingredients together until completely moist. Add a little water if the batter is too thick to pour into the ramekin. Tap the ramekin on the counter a couple of times to try to eliminate any bubbles.

Cook in the microwave for 50 seconds to one minute. Remove and set on counter to cool. Gently press against the muffin to rock it free from the container. Let cool until you can touch the ramekin without burning your fingers, then gently tap it and turn upside down to release the muffin. If it doesn't come out easily, push against the sides of the muffin and continue to tap the bottom. If it still will not release, slide a knife along the sides and gently nudge the bottom until it pulls free. Cut the muffin in half and toast, then butter and serve. Makes one muffin.

Nutrition Information per muffin:
 Calories: 225 Fat: 15.1 g Net Carbs: 3.5 g Protein: 12.9 g

Blueberry Magic Muffin

Everybody loves a blueberry muffin and even though the ones made with low-carb flour don't come close to the giant ones from the bakery, they are a satisfying substitute.

1 egg
1 tablespoon Coconut Oil (or other)
1 tablespoons Low-carb Flour
1 tablespoon Almond Flour
1/2 tablespoon Vanilla Whey Protein Powder (or use extra almond flour)
1 tablespoon Sugar Substitute
1 tablespoon Ricotta Cheese
10 Blueberries (dried) or fresh
1/2 teaspoon Almond Extract

In a one-cup ramekin or bowl, combine the egg, oil, sugar substitute, almond extract, and ricotta cheese. Using a whisk or a rubber/silicone spatula, mix together until well blended. Stir in the flour and protein powder until it is completely moist, then stir in the blueberries. I use dried blueberries to keep them from turning the muffin blue or purple, but fresh blueberries will work also.

Microwave for 45 to 50 seconds, then let cool for about five minutes. Sprinkle with a little powdered sugar and enjoy.

Nutrition Information per muffin:
Calories: 297 Fat: 26.1 g Net Carbs: 4.2 g Protein: 11.4 g

Note: If you use dried blueberries, dry them yourself. Most commercially dried fruits have added sugar in them. If you have a drier, you can spread them out on the drying pans and let the warm air-dry them for several hours until they are dehydrated.

Cheesy Magic Muffin Bread

This is a great bread to eat with Italian food or a salad. You can add your preferred cheese to it. I used Cheddar Jack, but it works with any sturdy cheese, such as Cheddar, Mozzarella, Swiss, or other grated cheese. It's also good for a hamburger bun or a sandwich. I prefer to make the microwave muffin, cut it across the middle, then toast it to get a slight browning on it.

1 Egg
1 tablespoon Olive Oil or other oil
2 tablespoons Low-carb Flour
1/2 teaspoon Baking Powder
Pinch Salt
1/4 cup Grated Cheese of choice
1/4 teaspoon Garlic Powder

In a bowl or mug, mix the egg with the oil until it is completely blended so no strings of egg white will show when it is cooked. Add the flour, baking powder, salt, and garlic powder. Mix together well, then stir in the cheese, mixing it through the batter.

Microwave for one minute, let cool a few minutes, then remove from the bowl. Slice, toast, and butter, then eat. Makes one muffin.

Nutrition Information per muffin (using 0 carb cheese):
 Calories: 338 Fat: 28.8 g Net Carbs: 3.3 g Protein: 16.5 g

Garlic Onion Magic Muffin Toast

Looking for a nice savory toast to put with hot wings or salad or a pizza sauce? This one might just do the trick. It uses garlic, onion, and Parmesan cheese to add to the flavor. It can also be a nice sandwich bun or melt cheese on top. Try building a hamburger on it or build your personal pizza, using pre-cooked meats and veggies, then bake in the oven or under the broiler about 8 to 10 minutes to melt the cheese.

1 Egg
1 tablespoon Olive Oil
1/2 tablespoon grated Parmesan Cheese
1 teaspoon dried Onion flakes
1 teaspoon minced Garlic
1 Green Onion, chopped
Dash of Garlic and Black Pepper
2 tablespoons Low-carb Baking Mix

In a bowl or mug, mix the egg, olive oil, Parmesan cheese, onion flakes, garlic, and green onions together until well mixed. Add a dash or a couple of twists of the pepper mill of the garlic and black pepper. Stir in the low-carb flour and mix together until it is blended into the batter. Tap the bottom of the bowl on the counter to try to get any air bubbles out.

Microwave for one minute. Let cool for about five minutes, then slice horizontally across the middle to make two slices of bread. Put in the toaster and cook until browned the way you like your toast. You can also pop these under the broiler or into a toaster oven to toast. Butter and enjoy. Makes one large muffin.

Nutrition Information per muffin:
 Calories: 255 Fat: 21.3 g Net Carbs: 5.6 g Protein: 10.1 g

Cocoa Raspberry Magic Muffin Cake

A little lighter in taste than the heavier chocolate cake, this cocoa cake uses only one tablespoon of unsweetened cocoa powder to give it a creamy cocoa taste. The recipe makes two small cakes. I've topped it with raspberries because they're perfect together, but you can also use strawberries or another berry.

1 Egg
1 tablespoon Butter, melted
1 tablespoon Ricotta Cheese
1 tablespoon Powdered Cocoa Powder
2 tablespoons Low-carb Flour
1/4 teaspoon Baking Powder
12 fresh or frozen raspberries
1 tablespoon Heavy Cream
2 tablespoons Sugar Substitute

In a small bowl or a shake blender, add the egg, butter, ricotta cheese, cocoa powder, cream, and sugar substitute. Mix or blend until it is completely combined. Add the baking powder and flour, and mix until it is moist and no powder is left.

Pour 1/2 the mixture into each small ramekin, bowl, or cup. Top each container of muffin batter with six raspberries in the middle. Microwave for one minute, then check that it looks done or test it with a toothpick. If it is still moist, microwave another 15 seconds. Sprinkle powdered sugar substitute over the top and serve warm. Add a bit of whipped cream if you like. Makes two servings.

Nutrition Information per 1/2 recipe:
Calories: 149.4 Fat: 12.4 g Net Carbs: 2.9 g Protein: 5.9 g

Applesauce Magic Muffin Cake

Adding unsweetened applesauce to the mix adds a layer of apple flavor and more moisture to the muffin. I use a trick of cooking the muffin in the microwave for 45 seconds, then removing it from the mug or ramekin onto an aluminum foil covered pan with the muffin top down, then popping it into a 375-degree oven for about five minutes to finish the cooking and lightly brown it. It changes the taste and texture.

1 Egg
1 tablespoon Oil or Butter, melted
1 tablespoon Unsweetened Applesauce
1/2 teaspoon Ground Cinnamon
1/4 teaspoon Ground Cloves (optional)
2 tablespoons Low-carb Flour
1/2 teaspoon Baking Powder
1 tablespoon Sugar Substitute

In a microwaveable 3" to 4" bowl, mix the egg, oil, cinnamon, cloves, and sugar substitute together until blended. Add the flour and stir well with a rubber/silicone spatula or small whisk until the flour is combined with the moist ingredients.

Cook in the microwave for 1 minute, then let sit about 5 minutes to cool. This allows the muffin to set up well and not break easily. For extra pop, add 1/4 cup apple slices and arrange on top of batter before you cook it. Sprinkle a little sugar substitute and cinnamon on top. Makes one serving.

Nutrition Information per muffin:
Calories: 253.2 Fat: 21.9 g Net Carbs: 4.5 g Protein: 9.4 g
  (with apple slices, the carb count is about 7.2 to 8 grams depending on the apple type.)

Cinnamon Magic Muffin

Beginning with a basic magic muffin with cinnamon, this provides a simple batter bread that you can use in many ways. Cut it into slices and butter it, then eat. Toast it, butter, add low-carb jam, and eat. Or top it with a little peanut butter or a tablespoon of softened cream cheese, then add a little jam or sprinkle more cinnamon on top. You can also use it for French toast, as I did with the next recipe. Yes, you can have your French toast and still stay within your carb limits.

1 tablespoon Butter
1 Egg
2 teaspoons Sugar Substitute
1 teaspoon Cinnamon
2 tablespoons Low-carb Flour
1/2 tablespoon Vanilla Whey Protein Powder
1/2 teaspoon Vanilla Extract

Melt the butter, let cool a little, then add the egg, sugar substitute, vanilla extract, and cinnamon and stir together with a rubber/silicone spatula or small whisk. If you'd like, you can also use a drink blender to mix it. Add the flour and protein powder and stir in until it is well blended. Pour into a 1-cup ramekin or small bowl and microwave for 45 seconds. Remove and let cool a few minutes. If the batter appears too moist, microwave an additional 5 to 8 seconds.

Cut and eat with butter or jam or let it cool a little longer, then toast it.

Nutrition Information per muffin:
 Calories: 237 Fat: 19.9 g Net Carbs: 3.3 g Protein: 9.7 g

Magic Muffin Cinnamon French Toast

So, the really special thing to do with the cinnamon bread is to make French toast. Add a couple of slices of bacon and voilà, Sunday brunch. So start with the cinnamon muffin recipe on the previous page and make this delicious treat.

1 Basic Cinnamon Magic Muffin
1 Egg
1/2 tablespoon Heavy Cream
1/2 teaspoon Vanilla Extract
1/2 teaspoon Cinnamon
1 tablespoon Butter
1 teaspoon Powdered Sugar Substitute

Slice the muffin half across the middle and set aside. In a shallow pan or bowl, add the egg, heavy cream, cinnamon, and vanilla extract and stir together to blend. Dip each half of the muffin in the egg batter, coating on both sides. Let them sit for a few minutes before turning them over. They will absorb most of the egg.

Heat a non-stick skillet over a medium high heat, then add the butter and use a pancake spatula to spread it around the pan. When it is bubbly, add the slices of battered muffin and cook for a few minutes, then turn to the other side, and cook a few more minutes. The toast should have a nice browning on it and not be soggy.

Remove to a warm plate, butter, and sprinkle with powdered sugar substitute. Serve with sugar-free pancake syrup or sugar-free honey. Makes 1 serving.

Nutrition Information per serving (including muffin)
Calories: 442.5 Fat: 38.5 g Net Carbs: 4.2 g Protein: 16.1 g

Ricotta Magic Muffin Pancake

This is just one example of using the Magic Muffin recipe to create a pancake batter that works terrifically. You can also double it and make a waffle that serves two people.

1 tablespoon Ricotta Cheese
1 tablespoon Vanilla Whey Protein Powder (optional)
1 large Egg, fresh
1/4 teaspoon Baking Powder
1 tablespoon Canola Oil or Coconut Oil
2 tablespoons Baking Mix
1 teaspoon Sugar Substitute
1/2 teaspoon Vanilla Extract (optional)

If you don't use the protein powder, use an extra tablespoon of the baking mix or almond flour.

In a small bowl or blender, add the ricotta cheese, egg, oil, sugar substitute, and vanilla extract. Mix together until egg and oil are fully incorporated. Add dry ingredients. Mix until blended in. If the batter is too thick, add a little water. It should be easily poured out but not so thin that it will make a skinny pancake.

Heat a non-stick skillet and add butter or spray with baking spray. When the butter sizzles, add one-half of the batter and spread it around in a circle using a rubber/silicone spatula. If there is room in the pan, make the second pancake at the same time. Put a lid over the skillet and cook over medium heat until bubbles appear in the batter and it looks somewhat dry. This varies with the temperature of your flame, so check frequently. Use a pancake turner to flip the pancake and cook on the other side.

Cook the second pancake if you haven't done it already. Butter, stack, and serve with sugar-free Pancake Syrup. Several brands are available that have 0 carbs.

Nutrition Information per recipe:
 Calories: 252 Fat: 20.9 g Net Carbs: 3.1 g Protein: 11.7 g

To make a Waffle:

Double the pancake recipe above and mix well. Pour into a hot Belgian waffle iron and bake for about 2-1/2 minutes or until most of the steam has dissipated from the iron. Remove the waffle by flipping it from the iron onto your plate.

One-half waffle is one serving and the recipe makes a whole waffle. The carb count is the same as for the pancake. Butter and serve with sugar-free pancake syrup.

Sweet Nutty Magic Muffin

This is a cinnamon delight muffin with pecans sprinkled over the top before it is baked. Add a simple powdered sugar icing and it is a delectable treat.

1 Egg
1 tablespoon Butter, melted
1 tablespoon Ricotta Cheese
2 tablespoons Low-carb Flour
1 teaspoon Ground Cinnamon
1/2 teaspoon Ground Cloves
1 tablespoon Sugar Substitute
1/2 teaspoon Vanilla Extract
1 tablespoon Pecans or Walnuts, chopped

For the topping:
2 tablespoons Powdered Sugar Substitute
Splash of Vanilla Extract
1 to 2 tablespoons Water

In a small bowl, mix the egg, butter, ricotta cheese, and sugar substitute together until blended. Add the flour and spices and mix until combined.

Pour the batter into a 1-cup ramekin or large mug that has been sprayed with baking spray. Sprinkle the pecans in the middle. Microwave for one minute or until the muffin does not look moist in the center. If it is moist, then microwave another 10 seconds.

Let cool for about 5 minutes then run a knife around the edges. Place a saucer over the ramekin and flip, tap the bottom a few times, and it should be on the saucer. Carefully turn the muffin to the correct side up.

Mix the powdered sugar, vanilla, and 1-tablespoon water in a small saucer or bowl. Add enough water to make it a syrup consistency, then spoon it over the top of the muffin.

Serves one. If you wish to divide it in half, it will make two average-sized muffins. You can cook it in two 1/2 cup ramekins for about the same time in the microwave.

Nutrition Information per muffin:
Calories: 350 Fat: 28.9 Net Carbs: 5.7 g Protein: 12.7 g

Lemon Cheese Magic Muffin Cake

So good and a snap to make. This can be a breakfast treat or a nice dessert. The key to its light, moist texture is cream cheese. Trust me, this is scrumptious.

1 ounce Cream Cheese
1 tablespoon Butter
1 teaspoon Sugar-free Lemonade mix
1/4 teaspoon Lemon Juice
1 tablespoon Sugar Substitute
1 Egg
2 tablespoons Low-carb Flour
1/4 teaspoon Baking Powder

In a 1 cup ramekin or a mug, put the cream cheese and butter. Microwave for 15 seconds to soften. Add the lemonade mix and egg and stir together with a rubber/silicone spatula until well blended. Add the lemon juice and sugar substitute and stir again. Then add the flour and baking powder, and mix until completely combined.

Microwave for 50 seconds. Let sit and mix a powdered sugar glaze to put on top.

Use one tablespoon sugar-free powdered sugar, a pat of butter, and about 1/4 teaspoon cream and mix together well. Add a little water if it is too thick. Spread over the top of the cake. Makes one cake.

Nutrition Information per cake:
Calories: 295 Fat: 26.3 g Net Carbs: 3.9 g Protein: 10.5 g

Peanut Butter Chocolate Chip Magic Muffin

Look for the lowest carb creamy peanut butter you can find. Mine came to about 1.8 net carbs for a tablespoon. These vary quite a bit based on manufacturer. The muffin is light and moist with a hint of peanut butter flavor and the bursts of chocolate from the chips. A sprinkle of powdered sugar substitute over the top adds just a touch more sweetness to it.

1 Egg
1 tablespoon Low-carb Flour
1 tablespoon Flax Meal
1 tablespoon Peanut Butter
1 tablespoon Sugar-free Chocolate Chips
1 tablespoon Sugar Substitute
1 tablespoon Butter
1 teaspoon Powdered Sugar Substitute

In a bowl, mug, or one-cup ramekin, add the egg, peanut butter, butter, and sugar. Mix together well to really work the whites into the mixture. Add the flax meal and flour and stir it in well. It should be a thick batter. If it is too thick, add a little water. Microwave for ten seconds to melt the butter in and stir again. Add the chocolate chips and stir, then microwave for another forty to fifty seconds.

Remove and let cool a couple of minutes. The muffin should be moist. Run a knife around the edge and turn out onto a plate. Spread a little butter over the top, then sprinkle on the powdered sugar. Makes 1 big muffin or cut in half to share.

Nutrition information per muffin:
 Calories: 393 Fat: 32.9 g Net Carbs: 4.6 g Protein: 13.4 g

Pistachio Magic Muffin

While you can make this as a microwave muffin, the flavor is best when baked in an oven. I also make smaller muffins when I oven bake, so the portions are lower in carbohydrates. This recipe would make two of the microwave muffins instead of four cupcake-sized ones.

1/4 cup Egg whites (liquid) or 2 egg whites
2 tablespoons Ricotta Cheese, whole milk
1/4 package Sugar-Free Pistachio Pudding mix
2 tablespoons Canola Oil
1 tablespoon Heavy Whipping Cream
1/4 cup sugar Substitute
1/4 cup Low Carb Flour
1/2 teaspoon Baking Powder
1/2 tablespoon Vanilla Protein Powder (optional)

Preheat oven to 350 degrees (F.). Place four cupcake liners in a cupcake pan.

In a medium bowl, add the egg whites, ricotta cheese, pudding mix, sugar substitute, and cream and mix with a whisk until completely blended together. Add the oil and stir it in well. Add the flour, protein powder, and baking powder. Stir until the flour is blended in and completely moistened.

Put two tablespoons of batter into each cupcake well. If there is extra, divide it equally among the four. Add a little water into any empty wells so that they don't bake dry.

Bake for 25 to 30 minutes until the top is lightly browned and a toothpick inserted in the middle comes out clean. Let cool and serve or put in the refrigerator.

Nutrition Information per cupcake-sized muffin:
Calories: 123 Fat: 9.4 g Net Carbs: 3.1 g Protein: 5.5 g

To make one microwaved Pistachio muffin:

2 tablespoons Egg whites (liquid) or 1 egg white
1 tablespoons Ricotta Cheese, whole milk
2 teaspoons Sugar-Free Pistachio Pudding mix
1 tablespoons Oil
1/2 tablespoon Heavy Whipping Cream
2 tablespoons Sugar Substitute
2 tablespoons Low-carb Flour
1/4 teaspoon Baking Powder

Mix in a microwaveable bowl or cup. Tap the bowl or cup a couple of times on the counter to try to remove any air bubbles. Microwave for one minute and check that it is done and doesn't look liquid in the middle. If not, microwave another 15 seconds. Let sit at least five minutes, then run a knife around the edge and remove from the bowl or mug.

Sprinkle with a little sugar substitute on the top before eating.

Nutrition Information for one large muffin:
 Calories: 229 Fat: 18.9 g Net Carbs: 5.7 g Protein: 7.5 g

Pumpkin Pecan Magic Muffin

Pumpkin is one of the vegetables listed on the low-carb plan from the get-go. Smith's grocery stores make the best Pumpkin Chocolate Chip muffins I've ever gorged on. While I have bid farewell to those lovelies, I substituted in this one.

1 tablespoon Low-carb Flour
1 tablespoon Vanilla Whey Protein Powder
1 teaspoon Coconut Flour
1 Egg
2 tablespoons Pumpkin Puree
1 tablespoon Oil or melted Butter
1 teaspoon ground Cinnamon
1/4 teaspoon ground Cloves
2 tablespoons Sugar Substitute
Pinch salt
5 Pecan halves, broken into pieces (optional)

Preheat oven to 350 degrees (F.)

In a microwaveable bowl, break the egg and add the oil. Stir vigorously with a whisk or a thin spatula until the egg is well mixed. Add the seasonings, salt, and sugar substitute, and mix well. Then add the flour and nuts, if using. Stir until completely mixed.

Microwave for one minute. Let cool a few minutes. Prepare a baking pan by spraying with cooking spray. Turn the partially cooled muffin onto the pan. Bake for 5 to 6 minutes until lightly browned. Sprinkle with powdered sugar substitute or cinnamon and sugar substitute mix and serve warm or cooled. Makes one muffin.

Nutrition information per muffin:
Calories: 346 Fat: 33 g Net Carbs: 4.2 g Protein: 17.6 g

Butter Pecan Magic Muffin

This has to be one of the best-tasting muffins I've come up with, but then, I love pecans. Our house in West Texas had three huge pecan trees so I developed a real passion for them. When I moved to California, walnuts dominated the cooking, and while I like walnuts, I still prefer pecans. This works with either nut so use your preference.

2 tablespoons Low-carb Flour
1 Egg
1 tablespoon Butter, melted
1 tablespoon whole milk Ricotta Cheese
1 teaspoon ground Cinnamon
1/2 teaspoon ground Cloves (optional)
2 teaspoons Sugar Substitute

Topping
2 Tablespoons Pecans or Walnuts, chopped
1 tablespoon Butter
1 tablespoon Sugar-free Maple Syrup

In a 1-cup ramekin or mug, melt the butter and let cool for a few minutes. Add the egg and sugar substitute and stir well with a rubber/silicone spatula. Add the ricotta cheese and seasonings and mix in, then add the flour. Stir until it is blended into the mixture.

For the topping, put the chopped nuts on top of the batter in the ramekin, then swirl the maple syrup over the top. Cut the butter into pieces and distribute over the top.

Microwave for 45 seconds, then check for doneness with a toothpick. If the batter is moist, cook another few seconds until it is done. Let cool a few minutes, then serve with a sprinkle of powdered sugar substitute. Makes one muffin.

Nutrition information:
 Calories: 346.4 Fat: 31.5 g Net Carbs: 3.0 g Protein: 12.0 g

For variety, you can also add in sugar-free chocolate chips; figure another .5 to the carb count if you use about 2 tablespoons.

Or you can add in 2 tablespoons chopped fresh cranberries and add a tablespoon of sugar substitute to balance the tartness. This adds about 1.2 net carbs.

Other options include 1/4 small apple, chopped or 2 tablespoons blueberries or raspberries added into the batter. A fourth of an apple adds about 3 net carbs to the muffin. Blueberries add about 2 net carbs while raspberries add less than 1 net carb.

Special Ingredients

While I have tried to avoid using too many special ingredients in this cookbook, there are some, and they may be optional in the recipes. I am trying to keep the recipes as low in carbs as possible and this involves using ingredients that are manufactured with low-carb dieters and diabetics in mind. In baking, the flours used are either nut flours or ones that are greatly reduced in wheat to create low-carb flours. While these don't taste exactly like the commercially produced flours, they make a bread product that is tasty and still good for you.

Flours
Several manufacturers create low-carb baking mixes and flours. Among them are:
Tova Foods – makers of Carbolose and CarbQuick Baking Mix
LC Foods – makers of many types of flours and mixes to help make low-carb, gluten-free baked goods, including cookies, cakes, and bread. They also sell low-carb jams and other products.
Dixie Carb Counters – makers of their own baking mix, many package mixes for bread, cheesecake, cookies and other meals. I recently found that their baking mix, Bakesquick, has a finer quality than Tova Foods' mix. I prefer it for making these muffins and cakes. It is a little more expensive than CarbQuick, but worth it.
New Hope Mills – makers of three fabulous muffin bread mixes and pancake mixes. I keep hoping they will expand their low-carb line.
NOW Foods – makers of almond flour and coconut flour as well as other baking products.
Bob's Red Mill – a mill that you might find in your local grocery store. BRM produces almond flour, soy flour, hazelnut flour, low-carb baking mix, flax meal, and other grains.
Ideal Foods – makes almond flour, flax meal, and several other flours that are sold in grocery stores.

All Low-carb flours are not created equal. Check the net carb (total carbohydrates minus fiber) count on the flours before using them. I generally use the lowest ones I can find, so if you use a baking mix that is 5 net carbs for 1/2 cup, then you'll be 2 carbs higher on the whole recipe than I am. As it is, the nutrition information may vary a little depending on how you measure, how large a particular fruit may be, and how you divide the dough up when baking.

Sugars
Sugar substitutes are controversial and are often in the news as not being all that good for you. I can only counter with the realization that sugar isn't that good for you either, especially when it packs the pounds on. You can completely give up sugar, but it's not easy to bake anything without some sweetener in it. Honey, agave, and any of the other syrups offered as a replacement are not low-carb and are processed the same as sugar in your body.

There are quite a few brands of sweetener on the market. Generally, if the package is pink, it is a saccharin-based sweetener. If it is blue, then it is aspartame-based. A yellow package is sucralose-based, and if it is green, then it tends toward stevia.

Recently, sugar alcohols have come into the market, but they aren't found easily at the grocery store. They are not actually an alcohol, but a product extracted from sugar. They are 0 calories and 0 carbs, but they don't agree with everyone's digestive system. Too much can cause stomach upset, so it's best to mix it with other sugar substitutes.

One of the things to keep in mind with any of the sugar substitutes, except the sugar alcohols, is that the actual sweetener is 0 carbs, but the medium used to carry the product—the powder in the package—has a little bit less than 1 gram, of carbohydrate in it. It isn't a problem when you don't use it often, but if you are baking with it, a half cup of sugar substitute can add a few carbs to the count.

Powdered or confectioners' sugar substitutes are hard to find. LC Foods makes one that tastes very good, but I have had a little trouble with it setting up too fast when making a sugar and cream icing, and it becomes gummy. Swerve also makes sugar substitutes in both granular and powdered form. You can make your own by putting about four times the amount of granulated sugar substitute you need into a blender and processing until it is a fine powder.

Other Baking Products

Some of the other powders and grains I use in my baking are low-carb products that add texture and additional flavor to the finished goods. Among these:

Whey Protein Powder adds more protein, texture, and flavor to bread products as well as making low-carb shakes. It comes unflavored and in vanilla, chocolate and strawberry. It is not inexpensive, but I use only a tablespoon or two in baking. Look for the lowest carb one you can find. Mine is 1 net carb per scoop (about 1/4 cup).

Oat Fiber adds texture and maybe a bit of flavor, but it isn't noticeable. It also adds more fiber to the baked goods.

Egg White Powder adds more lift to the baked goods, but you can accomplish this by adding an egg white to the mix instead of the powder. When baking with coconut flour, extra egg whites are required if you want it to rise at all. Baking powder and baking soda have no effect on coconut flour.

Sugar-free Chocolate Chips, made by Hershey's, are usually available at Wal-Mart stores. Most of the other grocery stores in my town don't carry them. Other ones are available by order from various sources.

Sugar-free Syrups are made by several manufacturers and are great add-ins to your coffee and your cooking. You can find them in many grocery stores although better prices might be found from on-line vendors.

That said, I wish you all happy cooking and hope that this cookbook will open up some new possibilities for you. Please check out my blog [http://reneaverett.me/skinnygirl/] for more recipes and look for more cookbooks in this series in the future.

Conversion Tables

A few conversion tables to help non-Americans figure out the measures.

Measurement Conversions

Measure	Equivalent
1/8 cup	2 tablespoons
1/4 cup	4 Tablespoons
1/3 cup	5 Tablespoons plus 1 teaspoon
1/2 cup	8 Tablespoons
3/4 cup	12 Tablespoons
1 cup	16 Tablespoons
1 Pound	16 ounces
8 Fluid ounces	1 Cup
1 Pint	2 Cups (= 16 fluid ounces)
1 Quart	2 Pints (= 4 cups)
1 Gallon	4 Quarts (= 16 cups)

Figure 1. Measurement Conversion Table

Food Measures

Measure	Equivalents	
Butter		
1 T.	14 grams	1 Tablespoon
1 stick	4 ounces=113 grams	8 tablespoons = 1/2 cup
Lemon		
1 lemon	1 to 3 tablespoons juice, 1 to 1½ teaspoons grated zest	
4 large lemons	1 cup juice	1/4 cup grated zest
Chocolate		
1 ounce	¼ cup grated 40 grams	
6 ounces chips	1 cup chips 160 grams	
cocoa powder	1 cup 115 grams	
Creams		
Half and half	½ milk ½ cream	10.5 to 18 % butterfat
Light cream		18 % butterfat
Light whipping cream		26-30 % butterfat
Heavy cream	whipping cream	36 % or more butterfat

Figure 2. Food Measure Table

Measures for Pans and Dishes

Inches	Centimeters
9-by-13-inches baking dish	22-by-33-centimeter baking dish
8-by-8-inches baking dish	20-by-20-centimeter baking dish
9-by-5-inches loaf pan (8 cups in capacity)	23-by-12-centimeter loaf pan (2 liters in capacity)
10-inch tart or cake pan	25-centimeter tart or cake pan
9-inch cake pan	22-centimeter cake pan

Figure 3. Measures for Pans and Dishes Table.

About the Author

Rene Averett blogs regularly on her **Skinny Girl Bistro** site where she shares information about low-carb foods, living a low-carb lifestyle, and many recipes. This book combines the first three booklets in the *Low-carb 15* series. She also has two books in the *Low-carb Recipe Magic* series.

Born in Texas, Rene has been transplanted and thrives in Nevada. She has lived in Los Angeles and Las Vegas and now makes her home in Reno, Nevada. The latter part of her career centered on doing technical writing for a large gaming manufacturer, and she enjoyed it right up until her retirement. She is now pursuing a career as an author and book publisher under Pynhavyn Press. She is a member of the Fiction Writers Group and the High Sierra Writers.

She loves the view of both the beautiful Sierra Nevada Mountains and the Virginia City Foothills from her house in South Reno that she shares with her long time companion, a Bichpoo dog, and two longhaired felines. In addition to cooking, she attempts a bit of gardening, plays the guitar, and loves to read. She writes fantasy, urban fantasy, and paranormal suspense novels as Lillian I. Wolfe and suspense romance under Riona Kelly. She has also published her first two children's books.

Feedback is welcome. You can contact her via her website at: http://reneaverett.me/skinnygirl/ or at mailto:Rene@pynhavyn.com

You can also connect at her Facebook page, Skinny Girl Bistro at: https://www.facebook.com/sgbistro
Her Twitter account is: http://twitter.com/neelaban

If you enjoyed this book and found it helpful, please consider leaving a review to help other people discover it. Thank you.

www.ingramcontent.com/pod-product-compliance
Lightning Source LLC
Chambersburg PA
CBHW031354060726

47590CB00007B/2776